The Inspection Panel

International Bank for Reconstruction and Development
International Development Association

Annual Report

August 1, 2000 to July 31, 2001

Published for the Inspection Panel

The World Bank
Washington, D.C.

The Inspection Panel
1818 H Street, N.W.
Washington, D.C. 20433
USA

Telephone: 202-458-5200
Facsimile: 202-522-0916
Internet: www.inspectionpanel.org
E-mail: ipanel@worldbank.org

© 2001 The International Bank for Reconstruction
and Development / The World Bank
1818 H Street, N.W.
Washington, D.C. 20433 USA

All rights reserved
Manufactured in the United States of America
First printing September 2001

Printed on recycled paper

A free publication

Contents

Abbreviations and Acronyms	iv
Letter of Transmittal	1
Message from the Panel	3
The Inspection Panel	5
Formal Requests Received in Fiscal 2001	9
Request No. 22, Chad: Petroleum Development and Pipeline Project	9
Request No. 23, India: Coal Sector and Social Mitigation Project	12
Action on Earlier Requests	15
Request No. 19, Kenya: Lake Victoria Environmental Management Project	15
Request No. 20, Ecuador: Mining Development and Environmental Control Technical Assistance Project	18
Operations	21
Outreach and Disclosure	29
Administration and Budget	33
Annex 1: Resolution No. IBRD 93-10, Resolution No. IDA 93-6, "The World Bank Inspection Panel"	35
Annex 2: 1996 Clarification of Certain Aspects of the Resolution	40
Annex 3: 1999 Clarification of the Board's Second Review of the Inspection Panel	43
Annex 4: Operating Procedures	47
Annex 5: Panel Budget	65

Boxes

Box 1: Inspection Panel Members	7
Box 2: Chad / Cameroon Petroleum Development and Pipeline Project	10
Box 3: Chad: Country Information	11
Box 4: The Coal India Environmental and Social Mitigation Project and the Coal Sector Rehabilitation Project	13
Box 5: Parej East Coal Mine	13
Box 6: Lake Victoria Environmental Management Project	16
Box 7: Lake Victoria	17
Box 8: Ecuador Mining Development and Environmental Control Technical Assistance Project	19

Tables

Table 1: Summary of Request for Inspection Projects in Chad	11
Table 2: Summary of Requests for Inspection as of July 2000	21
Table 3: Alleged Violations of Policies and Procedures	26

Figures

Figure 1: Inspection Panel Eligibility Phase	6
Figure 2: Inspection Panel Investigation Phase	6
Figure 3: Percentage of Requests Received by Region	27
Figure 4: Times Requesters Claimed Violation of Safeguard Policies	28

Abbreviations and Acronyms

BP	Bank Procedures
COTCO	Cameroon Oil Transportation Company
CSESMP	Coal Sector Environmental and Social Mitigation Project
CSRP	Coal Sector Rehabilitation Project
DECOIN	Defensa y Concervación Ecológica de Intag
EA	Environmental Assessment
ECOVIC	East African Communities Organization for Management of Lake Victoria Resources
IBRD	International Bank for Reconstruction and Development
IDA	International Development Association
IFC	International Finance Corporation
LVEMP	Lake Victoria Environmental Management Project
MOP	Memorandum of the President
NGO	Nongovernmental Organization
OD	Operational Directive
OP	Operational Policy Statement
OPN	Operations Policy Note
OSIENALA	Friends of Lake Victoria
PID	Project Information Document
PRODEMINCA	Proyecto de desarollo Minero y Control Ambiental
RECONCILE	Resources Conflict Institute
SAR	Staff Appraisal Report
TOTCO	Tchad Oil Transportation Company

Letter of Transmittal

This Annual Report, which covers the period August 1, 2000 to July 31, 2001, has been prepared by the members of the Inspection Panel for the International Bank for Reconstruction and Development and the International Development Association in accordance with the Resolution that established the Panel. The Report is being circulated to the Executive Directors and President of both institutions.

The Panel would like to take this opportunity to express its sincere gratitude and appreciation to the Executive Directors for their unfailing support. The Panel would also like to thank Senior Management, Bank staff, and especially the President, James D. Wolfensohn, for their cooperation and support in helping to make the Panel's function an integral component of the Bank's transparency and accountability efforts.

On a sadder note, we mourn the passing of Mr. Ibrahim F. I. Shihata, (former General Counsel and Senior Vice President of the World Bank) who was instrumental in the creation of the Panel, and who published the first book on the Panel.

Jim MacNeill
Chairman

July 31, 2001

Message from the Panel

The Inspection Panel concluded its seventh year of operation on July 31, 2001. This year, the Panel completed work on two Requests for Inspection and received two more. It began work on the overdue revisions of its 1994 Operating Procedures. And, in response to the Executive Directors' stated desire to make the Panel better known, it reinforced its outreach efforts.

During the year, the Panel completed two investigations authorized by the Executive Directors under the 1999 Clarifications to their 1993 Resolution. To date, three investigations have been approved under the 1999 Clarifications: the first was related to the Qinghai component of the China Western Poverty Reduction Project, which was completed last year. The two investigations this year were related to the IDA/GEF-financed WaterHyacinth Control Component of the Kenya Lake Victoria Environmental Management Project and the IBRD-financed Ecuador Mining Development and Environmental Control Technical Assistance Project. As discussed in this report, in both of these cases, Management responded with recommendations to the Board to deal with the problems identified in the Panel's findings as required by the Resolution.

The Panel also registered two new cases this year. It received a Request concerning the Chad portion of the Chad Petroleum Development and Pipeline Project, and another concerning the effects of a coal mine rehabilitation under the India Coal Sector Environmental and Social Mitigation Project. Both are discussed in this report.

This year's requests were generally typical of the Panel's experience. To date, it has dealt with 23 formal Requests for Inspection, including seven from Africa, seven from South Asia, eight from Latin America, and one from East Asia. In most of these cases, Requesters have alleged violations of some of the Bank's safeguard polices, especially Environmental Assessment, Involuntary Resettlement, Indigenous Peoples, and Disclosure of Information, as well as of the Bank's Operational Directive on Project Supervision. In addition, issues of consultation or participation—or the lack thereof—have frequently been raised.

Of the 23 formal Requests received, the Panel has recommended investigations in a total of nine cases, six under the rules which applied prior to the April 1999 Clarifications and three since. The Board approved only two of the six recommended investigations under the old rules. And both of them, the 1994 investigation of the proposed Arun III Hydroelectric Project in Nepal, and 1997 investigation of the NTPC Power Generation Project in India, were limited in scope. Indeed, the NTPC investigation took the form of a desk study in Washington. Since the 1999 Clarifications, the Board has authorized all three investigations recommended by the Panel, and on a non-objection basis.

During the year, the Panel also began work on a revision of its Operating Procedures. As already noted, the Panel's mandate was established by the Bank's Executive Directors in 1993 when they adopted the founding Resolution. To give operational force to this Resolution, the Panel in 1994 wrote and adopted its first Operating Procedures. Nearly seven years later, these Procedures are in need of revision to reflect the Board's 1996 and 1999 Reviews of the Panel's functions. Revisions are also needed to reflect the lessons learned during the short history of the Panel. At the same time, the Panel would like to simplify its procedures to make them more understandable and accessible to the end users of the inspection mechanisms: people, usually poor, who may be adversely affected by Bank-financed projects. Since these Operating Procedures are prepared and adopted by the Panel, they can, of course, neither limit nor expand upon the terms of the Board-approved Resolution.

Before the Panel adopts any revisions to its Operating Procedures, it would like to have the benefit of extensive consultations. To that end, it has envisaged a consultation process similar to that followed by the International Finance Cooperation's Compliance Advisor Ombudsman before that office issued its operational guidelines. Therefore, the Panel has decided that during the course of the next year, it will seek the views of as wide a range of stakeholders as possible, including the Bank's Board of Executive Directors, those who have submitted Requests for Inspection in the past, Bank Management and Staff, national, regional, and international nongovernmental organizations, and academics and others who have expressed an interest in the work of the Panel.

The creation of the Inspection Panel was a watershed event not only in the Bank's history, but also in the evolution of international financial institutions. As the challenges of international development evolve, the work of the Inspection Panel remains important. Openness, accessibility, and accountability continue to be keys to sound development, and the demand for them continues. In the seven years since its establishment, the Panel has assisted the Bank in its efforts to increase the openness, accessibility, and accountability of the institution. It has provided a direct link between the Bank's highest governing body and the people its projects are intended to benefit. It has contributed to improving the consultative process available to people who have voiced concerns about the impact of Bank-financed projects. Its work has assisted the Bank in its efforts to increase compliance with its own policies and procedures. In all of this, the Panel has assisted the Bank in enhancing the scope of Bank accountability and increased the Bank's credibility in both its borrowing and non-borrowing member countries.

Panel members (left to right): Jim MacNeill, Maartje van Putten, and Edward S. Ayensu

Jim MacNeill
Edward S. Ayensu
Maartje van Putten

The Inspection Panel

The World Bank created the Inspection Panel in 1993, on the eve of its 50th anniversary, to serve as an independent mechanism to ensure accountability in Bank operations with respect to its policies and procedures.[1] It was an unprecedented act in the history of international financial institutions. Since its inception, the Panel has provided people affected by Bank financed projects with direct access to an international forum where their complaints can be addressed. After almost five years of the Panel's operation, in April 1999, the Board confirmed "the importance of the Panel's function, its independence and integrity." [2]

Subject to Board approval, the three-member Panel is empowered to investigate problems that are alleged to have arisen as a result of the Bank having not complied with its own operating policies and procedures in the design, appraisal, or supervision of the projects it finances. As directed by the Resolution that established the Panel, the Executive Directors reviewed the Panel's experience after two years of operations. The review was concluded on October 17, 1996 with the approval of certain Clarifications of the Resolution. In March 1998, the Board launched a second review of the Panel's operations, which ended in April 1999 with the approval of the second Clarifications of the Resolution (see Annex 1,2, and 3, respectively, for the full texts of the Resolution and the 1996 and 1999 Clarifications).

Panel Process

The Panel's process is very straightforward. Any two or more individuals or groups of individuals who believe that they or their interests have or are likely to be harmed by a Bank-supported project can request the Panel to investigate their complaints. After the Panel receives a Request for Inspection, it is processed as follows:

- The Panel decides whether the Request is prima facie not barred from Panel consideration.
- The Panel registers the Request—a purely administrative procedure.
- The Panel promptly notifies the members of the Board that a Request has been received, sends the Request to them and to Bank Management.
- Bank Management has 21 working days to respond to the allegations of the Requesters.
- Upon receipt of Management's Response, the Panel conducts a 21 working-day review to determine the eligibility of the Requesters and the Request.
- The Panel delivers its eligibility report and any recommendation on an investigation to the Board.
- If the Panel does not recommend an investigation, and the Board accepts that recommendation, the case is considered closed. The Board, could nevertheless, decide and instruct the Panel to make an investigation.
- After the Board's approval of the Panel's recommendation, the Requesters are notified.
- Shortly after the Board decides whether an investigation should be carried out, the Panel's Report (including the Request for Inspection and Management's Response) is publicly available at the Bank's InfoShop and the respective Bank Country Office, as well as on the Panel's website (*www.inspectionpanel.org*).
- If the Panel recommends an investigation, and the Board approves it,[3] the Panel undertakes a full investigation. The investigation is not time-bound.

---

[1] See Resolution No. IBRD 93-10; Resolution No. IDA 93-6, establishing "The World Bank Inspection Panel." The Panel's 1994 "Operating Procedures" provide detail to the Resolutions. For the purposes of the Inspection Panel, the "World Bank" comprises both the International Bank for Reconstruction and Development (IBRD) and the International Development Association (IDA).

[2] *Conclusions of the Board's Second Review of the Inspection Panel* (hereinafer "1999 Clarifications"), IBRD and IDA Board of Executive Directors, April 20, 1999, paragraph 1.

[3] Id., paragraph 9.

INSPECTION PANEL ANNUAL REPORT 2000-2001

- When the Panel completes an investigation, it sends its findings on the matters alleged in the Request for Inspection to the Board and to Bank Management for its response to the Panel findings.
- Bank Management then has six weeks to submit its recommendations to the Board on what, if any, actions the Bank should take in response to the Panel's findings.
- The Board then takes the final decision on what should be done based on the Panel's findings and

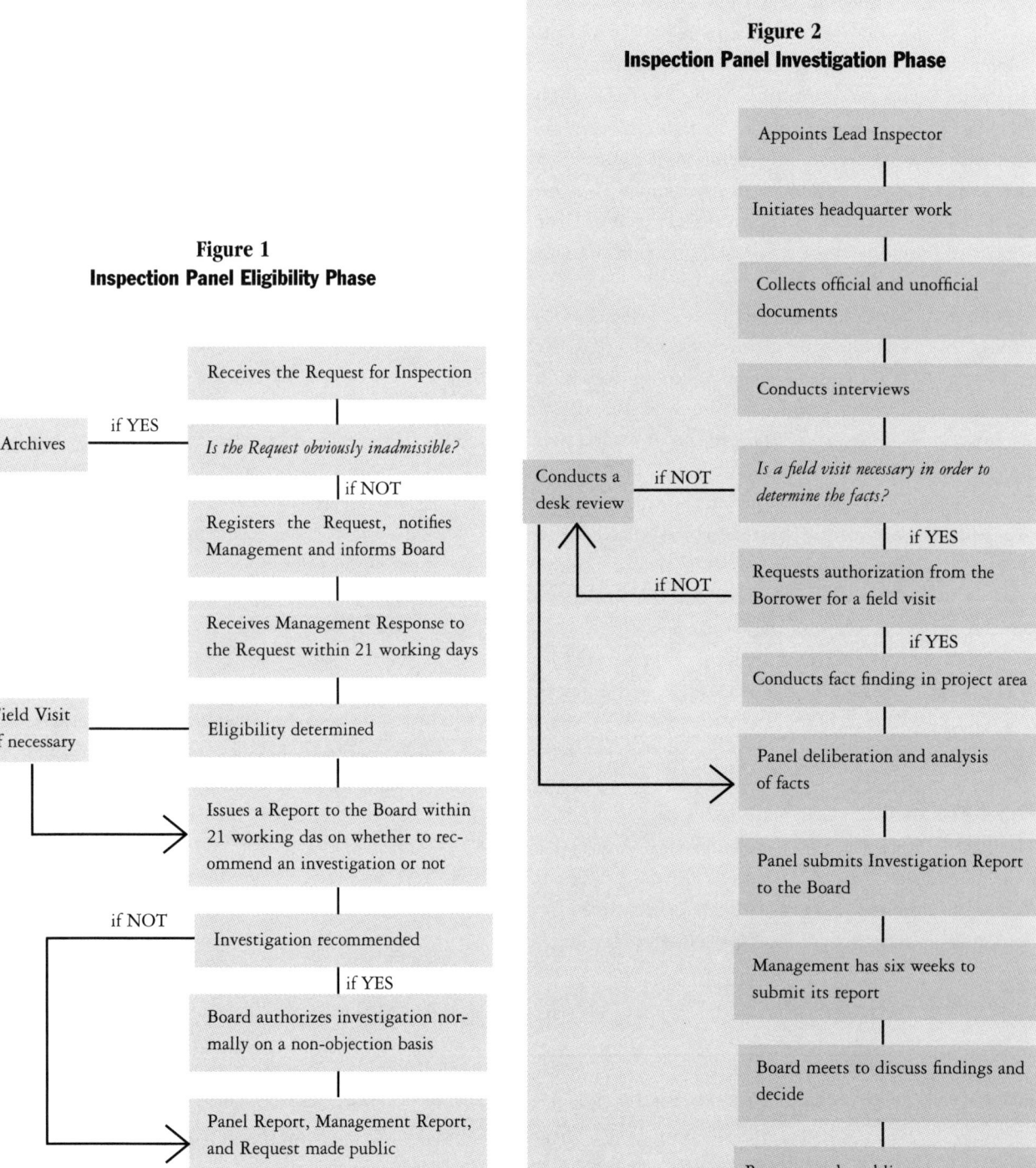

Figure 1
Inspection Panel Eligibility Phase

Figure 2
Inspection Panel Investigation Phase

BOX 1
Inspection Panel Members

Jim MacNeill, Chairman

Mr. MacNeill, a Canadian national, is a policy advisor on the environment, energy, management, and sustainable development to international organizations, governments, and industry. He is Chairman Emeritus of the International Institute for Sustainable Development, a member of the Boards of the Woods Hole Research Center and the Wuppertal Institute on Climate and Energy Policy, and a member of the Jury of the Volvo Environmental Prize. He was Secretary General of the World Commission on the Environment and Development (the Brundtland Commission) and lead author of the Commission's world-acclaimed report, "Our Common Future." He served for seven years as Director of Environment for the Organization for Economic Cooperation and Development (OECD). Earlier, he was a deputy minister in the Government of Canada. Mr. MacNeill holds a graduate diploma in Economics and Political Science from the University of Stockholm and Bachelor's Degrees in Science (Math and Physics) and Mechanical Engineering from Saskatchewan University. He is the author of a number of books, publications, and articles. He is also the recipient of a number of honorary degrees and awards, including the Order of Canada, his country's highest honor. Mr. MacNeill became a member of the Inspection Panel in August 1997.

Edward S. Ayensu

Professor Ayensu, a Ghanaian national, is the President of the Pan-African Union for Science and Technology; Chairman of Edward S. Ayensu Associates Ltd.; Executive Chairman of Advanced Gracewell Communications Co. Ltd.; founding Chairman of the African Biosciences Network, and formerly the Secretary-General of the International Union of Biological Sciences; Chairman of the Ghana National Biodiversity Committee; member of the International Advisory Board on Global Scientific Communications, UNESCO; and member of the Board of Directors and International Vice-Chairman of the International Institute for Sustainable Development. Professor Ayensu is a fellow of various academies of arts and sciences. He has been Senior Advisor to the President of the African Development Bank and the Bank's Director for Central Projects. Previously he has held posts in international scientific organizations, including Director and Senior Scientist at the Smithsonian Institution, Washington, D.C. Professor Ayensu was a Visiting Fellow of Wolfson College, Oxford University, and Distinguished Professor of the University of Ghana, and twice the recipient of the Ghana National Science Award. He has a doctorate degree in the biological sciences from the University of London, and has published many books and articles on science, technology, and social and economic development of developing countries. Professor Ayensu was the recipient of the Outstanding Statesman Award in Ghana during the Millennium celebrations. Professor Ayensu became a member of the Inspection Panel in August 1998.

Maartje van Putten

Ms. van Putten, a Dutch national, was a member of the European Parliament until July 1999. She has been a highly active member of the Committee on Development and Cooperation for the past 10 years. Ms. van Putten has produced many outstanding reports on the effects of the GATT/Uruguay Round on the developing countries, fair trade, development aid for Asia and Latin America, the EU program for tropical forests and European policies toward indigenous peoples. She has extensive exposure to developing countries, and is active with nongovernmental organizations and extremely committed to the cause of development. Ms. van Putten has closely worked with the WWF European Policy Office as a key political partner to promote better EU conservation and sustainable development policies. She was also a consistently active member of the ACP (African, Caribbean and Pacific Group)-European Union Joint Assembly. Ms. van Putten was a freelance multimedia journalist for most of her professional career, and was a Senior Fellow of the Evert Vermeer Foundation from 1981 to 1989. She is the author of many articles and books on globalization, international division of labor and on gender issues. Currently a member of the European Center of Development Policy Management in the Netherlands, Ms. van Putten is President of the Board of European Network of Street Children Worldwide (ENSCW). She holds a HBO (bachelor) degree in community development from Sociale Academy Amsterdam, and a Diploma, Hoger Sociaal Pedagogisch Onderwijs (PVO) Amsterdam. Ms. van Putten became a member of the Inspection Panel in October 1999.

Bank Management's recommendations.
- Shortly after the Board's decision, the Panel's Report and Management's Recommendation are publicly available through the Bank's InfoShop and the respective Country Office.
- The Panel's Investigation Report is posted on its website (*www.inspectionpanel.org*).

Who Can Submit a Request for Inspection?
- A community of persons, including any two or more persons who share common interests or concerns regarding a Bank-supported project
- Local representatives on behalf of directly affected persons with proper proof of authorization
- A non-local representative, in exceptional circumstances where local representation is not available, could file a claim on behalf of local affected parties, and
- An Executive Director of IBRD or IDA.

About the Panel
The Inspection Panel consists of three members who are appointed by the Board for a non-renewable period of five years. As provided for in the Resolution that established the Panel, members are selected on the basis of their ability to deal thoroughly and fairly with the requests brought to them, their integrity and their independence from the Bank's Management, and their exposure to developmental issues and to living conditions in developing countries. A Panel member is disqualified from participating in the hearing of an investigation of any Request related to a matter in which he or she has a personal interest or has had significant involvement in any capacity. Panel members may be removed from office for cause, and only by decision of the Executive Directors.

The Panel's structure and operations further safeguard its independence. It is functionally independent of Bank Management, and reports solely to the Board. In addition, Panel members are prohibited from ever working for the Bank Group after their term ends.

Members
The members of the Panel are Jim MacNeill, (member since August 1997), Edward S. Ayensu, (member since August 1998), and Maartje van Putten (member since October 1999). Panel members are required to select their chairperson annually. The present chairman is Jim MacNeill. The chairperson of the Panel works full-time, and the two members part-time as needed.

Former members: Ernst-Günther Bröder (1994-1999), Richard Bissell (1994-1997), and Alvaro Umaña (1994-1998).

Secretariat
The Panel has a permanent Secretariat, headed by an Executive Secretary, Eduardo G. Abbot, a Chilean national. The office also consists of two Assistant Executive Secretaries, Antonia M. Macedo, a New Zealand national, and Alberto Ninio, a Brazilian national; a Program Assistant, Pamela Fraser, a Guyanese national; and a Team Assistant, Nimanthi Attapattu, a Canadian national. The Secretariat provides administrative support to the Chairman and Panel members, and assists the Panel in the processing of Requests, as well as responding to queries from potential Requesters. The Secretariat also coordinates other activities, such as research and information dissemination.

Formal Requests Received in Fiscal 2001

Request No. 22
Chad: Petroleum Development and Pipeline Project (Loan No. 4558-CD), Management of the Petroleum Economy Project (Credit No. 3316-CD), and Petroleum Sector Management Capacity Building Project (Credit No. 3373-CD)

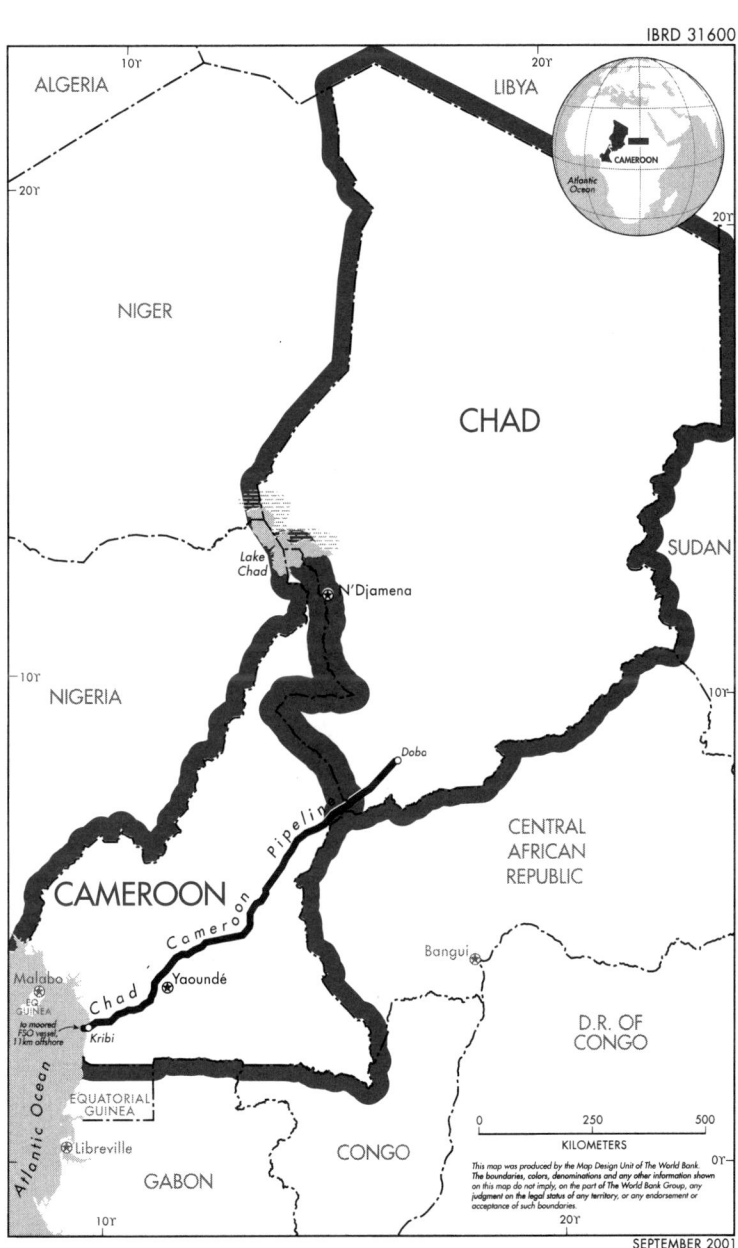

The Projects

The Chad Petroleum Development and Pipeline Project, the Management of the Petroleum Economy Project, and the Petroleum Sector Management Capacity Building Project (the Projects) form the overall package of assistance provided by the World Bank to Chad for the development of its oil fields as well as the institutional support for the implementation of a pipeline across Cameroon to the Atlantic Ocean. The Projects are part of the Bank's assistance strategy to support Chad's central development objective of reducing poverty by accelerating sustainable economic growth through the development of its petroleum reserves. The Projects are a part of the Chad/Cameroon Petroleum Development and Pipeline Project (see Box 2).

The Chad Petroleum Development and Pipeline Project is expected to generate over a billion dollars in royalties, dividends, and taxes for Chad over the 25-year production period, and substantially increase public resources for the country, facilitating additional expenditures for health, education, rural development, and infrastructure.

The Management of the Petroleum Economy Project aims to help Chad build its capacity to manage its oil revenues and to enable the country to absorb and allocate the expected oil revenue, effectively using such revenue for poverty reduction. The Project has five components: strengthening public financial management; creating a poverty database and strategy; developing human

> **BOX 2**
> **Chad / Cameroon Petroleum Development and Pipeline Project**
>
> The Pipeline Project is the largest construction venture in Sub-Saharan Africa. The sponsors of the Project are Exxon-Mobil of the U.S. (the operator, with 40 percent of the private equity), Petronas of Malaysia, and Chevron of the U.S., with 35 and 25 percent respectively. The Bank Group involvement and stated objectives are to support the development of a sound revenue management program, application of the Bank Group's strict environmental and social polices, and broad public consultations among all of the stakeholders in Chad and Cameroon. The Project is expected to cost about US$3.7 billion, of which 4 percent is funded by the Bank Group.
>
> The Project involves the drilling of 300 oil wells in the Doba Basin of southern Chad and the construction of a 650-mile pipeline from the wells through Cameroon to the Atlantic Ocean. The Project has three components: construction of the fields system (Part A), construction of the export system in Chad (Part B), and construction of the export system in Cameroon (Part C). It aims to assist in the development and export of the petroleum reserves of the Doba Basin oil fields in an environmentally and socially sound manner. The objectives of the Project are to increase government expenditures in Chad on poverty alleviation activities and to promote the economic growth of Chad and Cameroon through private sector-led development of Chad's petroleum reserves and their export through Cameroon. The Project could result in over US$1 billion in revenues for Chad, and is expected to provide resources to alleviate poverty by financing additional expenditures in health, education, rural development, and infrastructure. It would also provide needed additional Government revenues to Cameroon (as the transit country) of about US$500 million, which would be used to finance primary expenditures to support the country's macroeconomic stability.
>
> The Bank's Board approved financing for the Project on June 6, 2000. The Project was financed by IBRD Loans in the amount of US$39.5 million to Chad, and US$53.4 million to Cameroon, and IFC A-Loans in the amount of US$100 million, and B-Loans of up to US$300 million to COTCO and TOTCO, two joint venture companies established between the private sponsors and the governments of the two countries to own and operate the Chad and Cameroon portions of the export system.
>
> Source: Project Appraisal Document – Report No. 19343 AFR

resources; setting up oversight and control mechanisms; and monitoring economic reform and coordinating capacity building.

The Petroleum Sector Management Capacity Building Project aims to strengthen the capacity of the Government of Chad to manage the development of petroleum resources in an environmentally and socially sound manner, minimize and mitigate the potential negative environmental and social impacts of the Project on the producing region, and establish an effective framework for further private sector investment in the petroleum sector. The Project has two main components: the Doba Project Management Component, and the Petroleum Sector Management Component.

The Request

The Panel received the Request dated December 15, 2000 on March 22, 2001, and registered the Request on April 11, 2001. The Request was submitted by Mr. Ngarlejy Yorongar, who was acting for himself and on behalf of more than 100 residents living in the vicinity of three oil fields of the Doba Petroleum Project in the cantons of Miandoum, Komé, Béro, Mbikou, Bébédjia and Béboni, in the Bébédjia sub-prefecture of southern Chad. The Requesters asked that their names be made available only to the Panel. The Request focused mainly on the Chad portion of the Project.

The Request claimed that the Requesters' rights and interests had been, or are likely to be, directly harmed as a result of the Bank's actions in the design, appraisal, and supervision of the Projects. It alleges that the Bank's failure to comply with its policies and procedures on Environmental Assessment, Natural Habitats, Pest Management, Indigenous Peoples, Involuntary Resettlement, Forestry, Economic Evaluation of Investment Operations, Cultural Property, Disclosure of Operational

Information, and Project Supervision had resulted and would result in direct and adverse impacts on the Requesters. Among the impacts alleged were pollution and degradation of the environment, expropriation without compensation, lack of respect for the usages and customs of the Requesters, violations of their human rights, and bad governance reflected by the recent misappropriation of US$25 million and its use for the purchase of weapons.

In particular, the Requesters claimed that the development of petroleum activities, including development of the oil fields in southern Chad and the construction of an oil pipeline between Chad and Cameroon, represented a threat to local communities, their cultural property, and to the environment. Specifically, the Request claimed that people living in the Doba Basin were being harmed or are likely to be harmed because of the absence, or inadequacy, of compensation and environmental assessment. The Request claims that the Bank's monitoring and supervision policies and procedures were violated and that the Requesters' innumerable attempts to bring the problems associated with the Projects to the attention of Bank Management had not produced satisfactory results. Finally, the Request claimed that proper consultation with and disclosure of information to the local communities had not taken place. The Request also noted that the Requesters held the Bank accountable for what it had done as well as for what it had omitted to do.

Management Response/Panel Eligibility Report

Management submitted its Response to the Panel on May 10, 2001. The Panel's Eligibility Report to the Board was due on June 11, 2001. However, the processing of the Request coincided with the electoral and post-election process in Chad. Therefore, the Panel recommended that its report on the eligibility of the Request and its recommendation on whether or not to investigate be delayed for a period of about 90 days. The Board approved the Panel's recommendation for a 90-day extension on June 19, 2001. The Panel will submit its report and recommendation to the Board by September 17, 2001. The Request, Management Response, and the Panel's Report and Recommendation will be made public shortly after the Board has decided whether to authorize the inspection sought by the Requesters.

BOX 3
Chad: Country Information

Chad is one of the least developed and poorest countries in the world. Its key poverty indicators are well below Sub-Saharan African averages, and it was ranked 167th among 174 countries by the United Nations Human Development Index 2000, down from the UNDP's 1998 rating of 163. Chad's underdevelopment and poverty can be traced in large part to its difficult climate, landlocked position, and extended periods of civil strife. The country's growth and poverty reduction has been seriously hampered by a lack of financial resources and insufficient budget resources, which have forced the country to rely almost entirely on external financing for public investment. Chad, however, is endowed with considerable undeveloped petroleum resources, and the development and export of its petroleum reserves from the southwestern (Doba Basin) part of the country could significantly improve its development prospects.

An estimated 80 percent of Chad's population lives below the poverty line, and oil development would provide a major opportunity for the country to achieve its central development objective of reducing poverty by accelerating sustainable economic growth as well as providing financing for additional expenditures in health, education, rural development, and infrastructure.

Source: Project Information Document, Report No. PID7288

TABLE 1
Summary of Request for Inspection Projects in Chad

Project	Chad Petroleum Development and Pipeline Project	Management of the Petroleum Economy Project	Petroleum Sector Management Capacity Building Project
Financed by	IBRD Loan US$39.5 million	IDA Credit US$ 17.5 million equivalent	IDA Credit US$ 23.7 million equivalent
Sector	Energy	Public Financial Management	Energy / Petroleum
Board Approval Date	June 6, 2000	January 27, 2000	January 6, 2000

Request No. 23
India: Coal Sector Environmental and Social Mitigation Project (Credit No. 2862-IN) and Coal Sector Rehabilitation Project (Loan No. 4226-IN)

The Projects

The Coal Sector Environmental and Social Mitigation Project (CSESMP) is a package of high-priority environmental and social mitigations programs designed to help Coal India Ltd. (Coal India) strengthen its capacity to effectively alleviate environmental and social problems arising from mining activities, and to test the effectiveness of these policies in the 25 coal mines slated to receive financial support under the Coal Sector Rehabilitation Project (see Box 4). The programs included Resettlement and Rehabilitation Action Plans, Community Development Plans, and Indigenous Peoples Development Plans to safeguard the well-being of the project-affected people; Environmental Action Plans to minimize, insofar as possible, environmental degradation and restore mined-out lands to productive use; and the recruitment and training of Coal India staff to plan and implement the programs as it expands coal production to meet India's growing energy needs. The CSESMP became effective nearly two years earlier than the Coal Sector Rehabilitation Project (CSPR), in order to provide time for Coal India to develop the required capacity for environmental and social mitigation.

The CSPR was designed to support the Government's ongoing market-oriented coal sector reforms and to provide financial and technical support to Coal India's efforts to make itself commercially viable and self-sustaining. The Project also aimed to increase domestic supplies of coal by financing investment in 25 of the most profitable opencast mines of Coal India. The Parej East Coal mine, and the subject of the Request for Inspection is one of the 25 mines (see Box 5).

The Request

The Request for Inspection was submitted by Ms. Bina Stanis, of Chotanagpur Adivasi Sewa Samiti (CASS), a local nongovernmental organization (NGO) in the East Parej coal mining project area. The Request was submitted on behalf of residents in the project area who asked that their names be available only to the Panel. The Request was filed on June 21, 2001, and registered by the Panel on June 22, 2001.

The Request claimed that the Requesters' rights and interests had been adversely affected as a result of the Bank's violations of its policies and procedures on Involuntary Resettlement, Indigenous Peoples, Environmental Assessment, Disclosure of Operational Information, Management of Cultural Property, and Project Supervision. The Requesters claimed that they have suffered harm as a result of failures and omissions of IDA in the implementation of the CSESMP in the Parej East coal mine project area. They claimed that the Bank had failed to supervise the CSESMP adequately, as it had guaranteed to the projected-affected people when they had agreed to be resettled to allow for the proposed expansion of the Parej East mine subsequently financed by the Bank under the CSRP.

In particular, the Requesters claimed that failure to provide

Before involuntary settlement

BOX 4
The Coal India Environmental and Social Mitigation Project and the Coal Sector Rehabilitation Project

The two Projects, initially conceived as one, came about as a result of India's decision to continue its reliance on its coal reserves, and the Bank's support of the country's coal-based energy strategy. The foreign exchange and fiscal crisis of 1991 forced the Government of India to rethink the support it had traditionally given to chronically weak public enterprises such as Coal India, and to embark on a path of making the coal industry commercially and financially viable. Faced with budgetary constraints and huge investment requirements to meet the ever-increasing demand for coal, the Government started to phase out its budgetary support to Coal India during the period of 1993 to 1996. The Government asked for the Bank's assistance in 1993, and together with the Government and the management of Coal India, the Bank proposed an investment and technical assistance program that, in conjunction with the implementation of a program of reforms, was to safeguard both Coal India's financial viability in the future and initiate a process to make coal production in India environmentally and socially sustainable. Coal India produces about 90 percent of the coal supplies in India.

The original Coal Sector Rehabilitation Project contained financial and technical assistance for the implementation of Environmental Action Plans, Rehabilitation Action Plans, and Indigenous Peoples Development Plans. However, in May 1995, because of the scale and complexity of the mitigation measures, the Bank decided that the best way to address such issues comprehensively was to package the environmental and social components of the original Coal Sector Rehabilitation Project as a separate free-standing project, the Coal India Environmental and Social Mitigation Project (CSESMP).

The CSESMP was approved by the Board in May 1996, with financing by an IDA Credit of $US63 million equivalent. It became effective on July 23, 1996, with the proceeds onlent to Coal India. The closing date of the Credit was originally June 30, 2001, but the date was extended for one year, to June 30, 2002. The Coal Sector Rehabilitation Project (CSRP) was approved in September 1997 with financing by an IBRD Loan of US$530 million and an IDA Credit of about US$2 million equivalent. The Loan and the Credit became effective on June 17, 1998. However, on July 24, 2000, at the request of the Government of India, the Loan was reduced to US$261.3 million as a result of the cancellation of US$268.7 million from the undisbursed amounts of the loan, and the Credit was reduced to approximately US$1.41 million as a result of the cancellation of all amounts undisbursed as of that date. The closing date of the Loan and Credit is June 30, 2003.

Sources: MOP Report No. P-7104-IN; PID Report No. PID724

---

income restoration had resulted in significant harm and destroyed their livelihoods, and that now without compensatory land, employment and self-employment, they subsist as casual laborers living at mere survival levels. They also claimed a consequent loss of human dignity and demoralization at being dependent on the coal company that does not employ them. Formerly landowners, they now live in a colony without legal possession of any land, where their farming skills are no longer valued nor used. Their productive sources have been dismantled and their supporting networks and kin groups dispersed. They allege that they now suffer increased illnesses as a result of the pollution of water sources and wells in the resettlement

BOX 5
Parej East Coal Mine

Parej East Coal Mine is one of the 25 mines slated to receive financial support under the CSESMP and CSPR. It is an opencast coalfield located in the Hazaribagh District, Jharkand, a state created in August 2000 from the 18 southern districts of the state of Bihar. Parej East Coal mine is operated by Central Coalfields Ltd., a subsidiary of Coal India. The mine has been under development since 1993.

After involuntary settlement

colonies, and that there are no medical services to handle the increased illnesses, even though a dispensary was built, and they now lack the capability to acquire other services, such as education.

The Request asserted that there has been a lack of required consultation and participation, especially on changes made during the life of the Project to Coal India's Resettlement and Rehabilitation policy. The Request lists many violations of the Bank's policy on Involuntary Resettlement. Finally, the Request asserted that the self-employment Projects—which the Bank had guaranteed would compensate for the loss for land and livelihood—were grossly failing, and that the Requesters were unable to participate in the new economy around the mines. For this reason, they are suffering increasing poverty. The Requesters nonetheless called on Bank Management and the Board of Executive Directors to extend the CSESMP, with the remaining money targeted toward the restoration of the livelihoods of the project-affected people as well as environmental remediation.

Management Response/Panel Eligibility Report

The Panel received Management's Response to the Request on July 20, 2001. The Panel will submit its eligibility report and recommendation on whether to investigate to the Board no later than August 20, 2001. The Request, Management Response, and the Panel's Report and Recommendation will be made public shortly after the Board decides on whether to authorize the inspection sought by the Requesters.

Further Action on Earlier Requests

Chopping and shredding machine in operation

Request No. 19
Kenya: Lake Victoria Environmental Management Project (IDA Credit 2907-KE) (GEF TF 23829)

Background on the Request for Inspection Process

The Panel received the Request for Inspection on October 12, 1999, and registered it on November 22, 1999. The Request concerned one part of the water hyacinth management component of the Kenya Lake Victoria Environment Management Project (see Box 6 for background information on the Project). The Request was submitted by Resources Conflict Institute (RECONCILE), a Kenyan NGO, on behalf of the people living in the Nyanza Gulf area of Lake Victoria. RECONCILE was also authorized to represent OSIENALA, an NGO located in Kisuma, and the Kenyan Chapter of ECOVIC (the East African Communities Organization for Management of Lake Victoria Resources), an NGO representing the communities living along the Kenyan side of Lake Victoria. (See Box 7 for further details on Lake Victoria.)

The Requesters claimed that they were likely to suffer harm as a result of failures and omissions of IDA and IBRD (as the Administrator of GEF) in the design and implementation of the water hyacinth management component of the project. In particular, they claimed that the mechanical method for shredding water hyacinth in the Lake and allowing it to sink to the bottom would result in ecological and environmental degradation that would, in turn, adversely affect communities living on the Nyanza Gulf shores. They also claimed that the mechanical method was selected without a prior Environmental Assessment or appropriate community consultation.

Management submitted its Response to the Request on December 20, 1999. The Response noted that Management believed that the design and execution of the water hyacinth chopping and shredding pilot was completely acceptable, and that the Bank had complied with all relevant policies and procedures. The Panel found that the Request and the Requesters met the eligibility criteria as required by the Resolution, and recommended an investigation into the matters alleged in the Request on March 8, 2000. The Board approved the Panel's recommendation on April 10, 2000.

The Panel's Findings: The Investigation Report

The Panel found that Management was not in full compliance with Operational Directive (OD) 4.01, Environmen-

> **BOX 6**
> **Lake Victoria Environmental Management Project**
>
> Kenya, Tanzania, and Uganda share the management of Lake Victoria and its resources. The Lake Victoria Environmental Management Project (LVEMP) is a comprehensive five-year program aimed at the rehabilitation of the Lake's ecosystem for the benefit of the people living in its catchment. LVEMP was financed in July 1996 by an IDA Credit and GEF Grant, with the funds shared among the three countries. The Board of Directors approved an IDA Credit for US$12.8 million equivalent, and a GEF Grant for US$11.5 million equivalent to the Republic of Kenya.
>
> The main objectives of the LVEMP are to (a) maximize the sustainable benefits to the riparian communities by using resources within the basin to generate food, employment, and income, supply safe water, and sustain a disease-free environment; and (b) conserve biodiversity and genetic resources for the benefit of the riparian communities. In order to address the trade-offs among objectives that cut across national boundaries, a further project objective is to harmonize national environmental management programs in order to reverse, insofar as possible, increasing environmental degradation. The Project consists of two broad sets of activities. The first set addresses specific environmental threats, and is implemented in selected *pilot zones*. The second set of activities is *Lake-wide* in scope, and aims to expand information on the Lake and build capacity for more effective management.
>
> The goal of the water hyacinth control component of the LVEMP is to establish sustainable indigenous capacity to control water hyacinth, a noxious, rapidly growing weed that is responsible for increasing disease among the human population of the Lake Victoria Basin. The Kenyan part of the component included an experimental pilot that used mechanical chopping and dumping for fast removal of water hyacinth in an area where infestation was so great that it disrupted shipping, fishing, and livelihoods.
>
> Source: MOP Report No. P-6843 AFR

tal Assessment. It found that Management had made no prior review of the environmental consequences of the mechanical chopping and dumping method water hyacinth disposal, and that environmental and other data necessary for a subsequent assessments had not been obtained. The Panel also found that Management was not in compliance with paragraph 19 of the OD concerning consultations undertaken with the potentially affected people. The Panel also concluded that Bank Management was not in compliance with OD 13.05, Project Supervision, because supervision of the design and data collection systems for the pilot was inadequate, as was the supervision of the implementation of the monitoring systems.

With regard to categorizing the project a Category B for environmental assessment purposes, the Panel found that Management was in compliance with OD 4.01. The Panel also found that Management was in compliance with OD 4.15, and noted that even though it had witnessed some apparent harm to a small number of people engaged in the water hyacinth utilization industry, it was satisfied that that harm was not the outcome of the Bank's failure to comply with its policies and procedures. The Panel also noted that in its view, the social and economic benefits of the water hyacinth control

Kenyan children who live in the Lake catchment

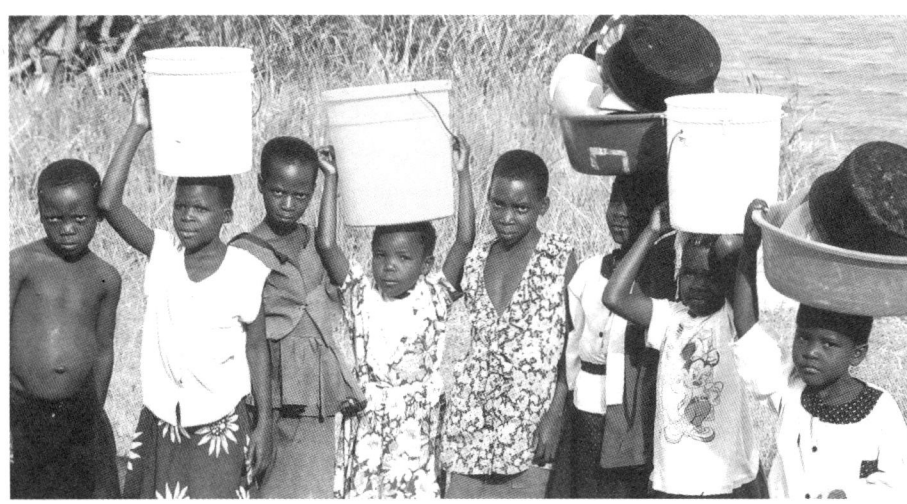

program had been significant and had been to the advantage of the overwhelming majority of the lakeshore dwellers. Furthermore, the Panel noted that Management was in compliance with Operational Policy (OP) 10.04, Economic Evaluation of Investment Operations, and stated that it was satisfied that in arriving at the mechanical shredding tender, Management had considered alternatives. Even though Management had not provided clear guidelines in terms of who would bear the cost of future shredding operations, the Panel noted that there was no evidence to indicate that the method would be unsustainable in view of the cost. The Panel sent its Investigation Report to the Board on December 28, 2000.

Management's Report and Recommendation
Following the Panel's Investigation Report, Management submitted its Report to the Board on April 20, 2001 indicating its recommendation in response to the Panel's findings. Management accepted the Panel's findings and recommended six actions: (a) continued monitoring of water quality in the area where the mechanical chopping took place; (b) vigilant surveillance and response to track the movement of large infestations and to project likely patterns of resurgence; (c) heightened community participation under the LVEMP; (d) cross-country participation in supervision missions to encourage the sharing of lessons from each country; (e) renewed activity of the Panel of Scientists to advise on scientific matters related to design

Water hyacinth plant

> **BOX 7**
> **Lake Victoria**
>
> As the world's second largest freshwater lake and the largest in the developing world, Lake Victoria sustains tens of millions of people. The annual gross economic product of the Lake catchment is about US$3 to 4 billion, and the catchment provides for the livelihoods of about one-third of the combined populations of the three riparian countries. With the exception of Kampala, the capital of Uganda, the catchment economy is principally agricultural, with a number of cash crops including fish exports. The lake's ecosystem harbors unique biological resources, and the Lake's basin is also used as a source of energy, drinking and irrigation water, shelter, transport, and as a repository for human, agricultural, and industrial waste.
>
> With the populations of the three riparian communities growing at rates among the highest in the world, the multiple uses have increasingly come into conflict. This has contributed to making the Lake environmentally unstable, and the Lake ecosystem has undergone substantial changes over the last three decades. Over-fishing and oxygen depletion at lower depths of the Lake threaten artisanal fisheries and the Lake's biodiversity, with more than 300 indigenous species facing extinction. Waterborne diseases have increased in frequency, and water hyacinth, absent as late as 1989, has begun to choke important waterways and landings.
>
> Sources: MOP Report No. P-6843 AFR; SAR Report No. 15429-AFR

activities supported by the project; and (f) a possible repeat of the pilot since Management agrees it is the only way to collect data for an adequate environmental impact assessment of the chopping method. Finally, Management noted that in the event of a repeat pilot, it would ensure that there would be full compliance with all the requirements in the relevant policies and procedures, and that funds would be available within the existing project envelope to cover the costs.

The Board's Decision
On May 2, 2001, the World Bank Board of Executive Directors approved the recommendations made by Bank Management in response to the Panel's findings.

Request No. 20
Ecuador: Mining Development and Environmental Control Technical Assistance Project (Loan 3655-EC)

Background

The Panel received the Request for Inspection on December 13, 1999, and registered it on December 17, 1999. The Request was submitted by DECOIN, an Ecuadorian NGO, on behalf of the people living in the Intag Area, and four representatives of the Associación de Caficultores Rio Intag. The Request concerned the geo-information subcomponent of the Ecuador Mining Development and Environmental Control Technical Assistance Project (see Box 8 for background information on the Project and subcomponent).

The Requesters claimed that the communities they represented were likely to suffer material harm as a result of failures and omissions by the Bank in the design and implementation of the Project. Specifically, they claimed that the public release of maps with mineral data collected under the Project's geo-information component would attract mining companies and informal miners, which, in turn would have a destructive impact on their communities and on the protected areas and buffer zones in the vicinity. They also alleged that Management failed to (a) consult and take into account the views of local communities and NGOs when preparing the environmental assessment; (b) consider the Project's impact on endangered ecosystems; (c) take into account the possible impact of divulging the information contained in the mineral maps; (d) assess the institutional ability of mining authorities to protect the areas from possible incursions of informal miners; (e) conform with Ecuadorian laws; and (f) properly monitor the Project.

Management submitted its Response to the Request on January 18, 2000. In its Response, Management noted that it considered that the Project was designed and appraised, and was being implemented and supervised, in compliance with all relevant Bank policies and procedures. Management further noted that it believed that the Requesters had failed to demonstrate actual or potential direct harm to their rights or interests as a result of the thematic mapping activities of the Project, since the Intag Valley, where the Requesters live had not been and was not going to be thematically mapped under the Project. Management added that the Requesters' claim of potential material harm from the possibility of future private mining operations in surrounding areas that had been or were to be mapped under the Project was speculative.

The Panel found that the Request and the Requesters met the eligibility criteria by the Board and, based on the Request and the Response, recommended on May 3, 2000 an investigation into the matters alleged in the Request. The Board approved the Panel's recommendation on May 15, 2000.

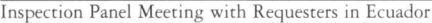

Inspection Panel Meeting with Requesters in Ecuador

FURTHER ACTION ON EARLIER REQUESTS

> BOX 8
> **Ecuador Mining Development and Environmental Control Technical Assistance Project**
>
> The Ecuador Mining Development and Environmental Control Technical Assistance Project (PRODEMINCA) was officially requested by the Government of Ecuador in 1989. PRODEMICA was financed by an IBRD Loan with cofinancing by the development agencies of the governments of Sweden and the United Kingdom. It was prepared between 1990 and 1992.The Board approved the US$14 million equivalent Loan on October 21, 1993. The Project closed in December 2000.
>
> The major objectives of PRODEMINCA were to (a) attract new private mining investment and support the systematic development of increased, but environmentally sound, mineral production; and (b) arrest mining-related environmental degradation and mitigate the damage resulting from the use of primitive and inadequate technology by informal miners.
>
> The Project comprised three major components: sector policy management, policy implementation, and project coordination. The policy implementation component, in turn, comprised three parts: mining and environmental health, management of mining rights, and geo-information. The Request focused specifically on the social and environmental consequences of the geo-information subcomponent.
>
> Source: MOP Report No. P-5988-EC

The Panel's Findings: The Investigation Report

The Panel found that Management was substantially in compliance with the provisions of OD 4.01, Environmental Assessment (formerly OD 4.00, Annex A); OPN 11.02, Wildlands (now OP/BP 4.04, Natural Habitats); and OD 13.05, Project Supervision. However, the Panel found that Management was in violation of certain provisions of the policies and procedures of OD 4.01 relating to processing, geographical scope, baseline data, and consultation during project preparation. The Panel sent its Investigation Report to the Board on February 23, 2001.

Management's Report and Recommendation

Management submitted its Report to the Board on April 28, 2001, indicating its recommendations in response to the Panel's findings. Management agreed with the Panel that it was substantially in compliance with OPN 11.02 and OD 13.05, and accepted the position stated in the Panel's Report that a more expanded and robust environmental assessment and consultation process should have been undertaken. Management did not propose any specific remedial efforts with regard to the claims made by the Requesters, but outlined actions and next steps in response to the Panel's findings. Management noted that even though the Project is closed, Bank staff will continue working with the Government and local NGOs implementing actions agreed on under the Project, especially with regard to the use of the geological and thematic mapping information produced by the Project. Management proposed that to prevent adverse social and environmental consequences and to ensure that information be used in favor of development effectiveness, there should be: (a) NGO participation in

Border of the Cotacachi-Cayapas Ecological Reserve

The Intag Valley

monitoring the use and application of the information generated under the Project; (b) strict enforcement of the license agreements for the use of such information; and (c) brochures published, and workshops held, on the use of geo-information. Management also outlined actions and next steps to be taken on the development of consultation mechanisms, support for conservation and environmental management, and the strengthening of environmental institutions.

The Board's Decision

On April 18, 2001, the Board of Executive Directors recorded their approval of the actions and next steps put forth by Bank Management for the Project.

Operations

TABLE 2
Summary of Requests for Inspection as of July 2001

REQUEST	REQUESTS REGISTERED	PANEL RECOMMENDATION / FINDINGS AND REPORTS SUBMITTED	BOARD DECISION	OUTCOME
#1 Nepal / Arun III Proposed Hydroelectric Project and Restructuring of IDA Credit	Yes 10/94	Investigation Recommendation Report 12/94 Investigation Report 6/95	Approved (2/95) The Board limited investigation to substantial complience with ODs 4.01 on Environmental Assessment, 4.20 on Indigenous Peoples, and 4.30 on Involuntary resettlement during the preparation and appraisal of the proposed project and implementation of a credit	On the basis of an independent study commissioned by the Bank, IDA President decided to withdraw financing for the Project
#2 Ethiopia / Exportation	No 5/95	The Request was found ineligible because the Requesters had not exhausted local remedies and had failed to establish how the lack of compensation was a consequence of any alleged acts or omissions by IDA (5/95)		
#3 Tanzania Emergency Power Project	Yes 6/95	**No investigation** **Recommendation Report 9/95** Bank found in compliance with IDA Articles of Agreement; Requesters found ineligible re: complaint on compliance with OD 4.01	Approved (9/95) The Board approved the Panel's recommendation on a non-objection basis	
#4 Brazil / Rondônia Natural Resources Management Project		Investigation **Recommendation Report 8/95** **Additional Review Report 12/95** **Review of Progress Report 3/97**	Not Approved (9/95) Initially, the Board decided that it could not make a decision without more factual information, and asked the Panel to conduct an Additional Review (9/95) After the Panel submitted its Additional Review Report and reiterated its recommendation for an investigation, the Board did not approve an investigation but asked the Panel to conduct a review of the progress in implementation of the project (1/97)	Partial concessions to affected people; limited Panel role in monitoring implementation
#5 Chile / Pangue / Ralco Complex of Hydroelectric Dams	No 11/95	Inadmissible because IFC is outside of the Panel's mandate, which is restricted to IBRD and IDA projects		The President appointed external consultants to investigate the matter

TABLE 2
Summary of Requests for Inspection as of July 2001, continued

REQUEST	REQUESTS REGISTERED	PANEL RECOMMENDATION / FINDINGS AND REPORTS SUBMITTED	BOARD DECISION	OUTCOME
#6 Bangladesh / Jamuna Bridge Project	Yes 8/96	No investigation **Recommendation Report 11/96** **Progress on Implementation Report 8/98** Panel found that the project's 1993 Resettlement Action Plan neither specifically identified nor provided assistance for char dwellers as project-affected people. But the Panel was satisfied that the Erosion and Flood Policy, issued Sept. 1996 (after the Request was filed) could constitute an adequate and enforceable basis for IDA to comply with its policies and address the char dwellers' concerns, thus making an investigation unnecessary	Approved (4/97) The Board approved the Panel's recommendation in Nov. 1996. But asked Management to submit a progress report on the implementation of the Revised Resettlement Action Plan and the Environmental Action Plan, and asked the Panel to assist the Board in a review of progress in 12 months	Project revised to respond to claim
#7 Argentina / Paraguay: Yacyretá Hydroelectric Project	Yes 10/96	Investigation **Recommendation Report 12/96** **Review of Present Problems and Assessment of Action Plans Report 9/97**	Not Approved (2/97) The Board asked the Panel to review the existing problems of the project in the areas of environment and resettlement, and to provide an assessment of the adequacy of the Action Plans agreed between the Borrower and the Bank to bring the project into compliance with Bank policies and procedures	Panel report found significant policy violations
#8 Bangladesh / Jute Sector Adjustment Credit	Yes 11/96	No investigation **Recommendation Report 3/97** The Panel found inadequacies in program design, but felt that further review through a formal investigation would serve no useful purpose	Approved (4/97) The Board accepted the Panel's recommendation on a non-objection basis	Bank halted funding
#9 Brazil / Itaparica Resettlement and Irrigation Project	Yes 3/97	Investigation **Recommendation Report 6/97**	Not Approved (9/97) The Board decided—given the government's action plan for completing the project, which included its own funding, and its Request for continued Bank supervision for two more years—that no investigation was needed and agreed to review progress on the Action Plan in 12 months with the Panel's assistance	Panel process bypassed
#10 India / NTPC Power Generation Project	Yes 5/97	Investigation **Recommendation Report 7/97** **Investigation Report 12/97**	Approved (9/97) After reviewing a remedial Action Plan submitted by Management in Sept. 1997, the Board approved an investigation, but restricted it to a desk study in Washington, D.C.	Management Action Plan approved by Board; local independent monitoring panel apointed

TABLE 2
Summary of Requests for Inspection as of July 2001, continued

REQUEST	REQUESTS REGISTERED	PANEL RECOMMENDATION / FINDINGS AND REPORTS SUBMITTED	BOARD DECISION	OUTCOME
#11 India / Ecodevelopment Project	Yes 4/98	Investigation Recommendation Report 10/98	Not Approved (12/98) The Board instructed Management to work with government officials at the state and federal level to find measures to address the Panel's initial findings, and to report back in six months. It was also agreed that the Panel would give its comments on Management's Report to the Board	Management asked to prepare a Status Report
#12 Lesotho / South Africa; Phase 1B of Lesotho Highlands Water Project	Yes 5/98	No investigation Recommendation Report 8/98 The Panel found no prima facie evidence linking the claims in the Request to the Bank's decision to proceed with financing of Phase 1B, but felt that Requester concerns about conditions on the ground were valid	Approved (9/98) The Board approved the Panel's recommendation on a non-objection basis	
#13 Nigeria / Lagos Drainage and Sanitation Project	Yes 6/98	No investigation Recommendation Report 11/98 The Panel found that most of the operational policies were followed during the preparation of the project. However, sociological considerations did not appear to be fully integrated into the project design and there was an absence of appropriate measures in the project design to ensure the effective maintenance of the drainage channels constructed under the project. The Borrower and IDA agreed on compensation measures for the resettlers identified by the Panel during its visit to the project site to ascertain eligibility of the Request	Approved (11/99) The Board approved the Panel's recommendation on a non-objection basis	
#14 Brazil / Land Reform Poverty Alleviation Project	Yes 1/99	No investigation Recommendation Report 6/99 The Panel found no evidence of harm, especially since the terms and conditions of the program's loans under the pilot program substantially improved after the Request was filed	Approved (6/99) The Board approved the Panel's recommendation on a non-objection basis	
#15 Lesotho / Highlands Water Project from Swissborough Diamond Mines Ltd & Others	Yes 5/99	No investigation Recommendation Report 7/99 The Panel found no direct link between any actions or omissions of the Bank with the harm claimed by the Requesters	Approved (8/99) The Board approved the Panel's recommendation on a non-objection basis	

TABLE 2
Summary of Requests for Inspection as of July 2001, continued

REQUEST	REQUESTS REGISTERED	PANEL RECOMMENDATION / FINDINGS AND REPORTS SUBMITTED	BOARD DECISION	OUTCOME
#16 China / Western Poverty Reduction Project	Yes 6/99	**Investigation** **Eligibility Report 8/99** The Panel found the Request met the eligibility requirement **Panel Findings** **Investigation Report 4/00** Management was substantially in compliance with the provisions of Annex B of OD 4.00 on Environmental Policy for Dams and Reservoir Projects, OP/BP 4.37 on Safety of Dams, BP 10.00 on Investment Lending: Identification to Board Presentation, and OP/BP 12.10 on Retroactive Financing, and in apparent violation of several provisions of OD 4.01 on Environmental Assessment, OD 4.20 on Indigenous Peoples, and OD 4.30 on Involuntary Resettlement, OP 4.09 on Pest Management, OP 10.00 on Investment Lending: Identification to Board Presentation, and BP 17.50 on Disclosure of Information	**Approved (9/99)** The Board, six days after the filing of the Request, approved financing for the project with the condition that no work would be done and no funds disbursed for the $40 million Qinghai component of the project until they decided on the results of any review by the Panel (6/99). The Executive Directors, after taking into account the Panel's recommendation, decided "as a Board" to instruct the Panel to investigate Management's compliance with certain policies and procedures. The Board met to consider the Panel's Investigation Report and Management's Response at a Board meeting on July 8-9, 2000. During the meeting the Borrower informed the Bank it would proceed with the component without Bank financing (7/00)	Finance request withdrawn for Qinghai component. The Borrower will continue Project with their own financing
#17 Argentina / Special Structural Adjustment Loan	Yes 8/99	**No Investigation** **Eligibility Report 12/99** The potential harm feared by the Requesters seemed to have been avoided by the favorable reaction of the Argentine authorities and Bank Management. Therefore, in the Panel's view an investigation was unnecessary	**Approved (1/00)** The Board approved the Panel's recommendation on a non-objection basis	
#18 Brazil / Land Reform Poverty Alleviation Project (2nd Request)	Yes 9/99	**Not Eligible / No Investigation** **Eligibility Report 12/99** The Panel was not satisfied that the Requesters had provided sufficient evidence that they had brought the matter to the attention of Bank Management as required by the Resolution. So the Request did not satisfy this eligibility criteria	**Approved (1/00)** The Board approved the Panel's recommendation on a non-objection basis	
#19 Kenya / Lake Victoria Environmental Management Project	Yes 11/99	**Investigation** **Eligibility Report 3/00** The Panel found the Request met the eligibility criteria	**Approved (3/00)** The Board approved the Panel's recommendation on a non-objection basis The Board approved Management recommendations on a non-objection basis on May 2, 2001	Management accepted Panel findings and recommendations. The following six actions were recommended: (a) continued monitoring; (b) vigilant surveillance,

OPERATIONS

TABLE 2
Summary of Requests for Inspection as of July 2001, continued

REQUEST	REQUESTS REGISTERED	PANEL RECOMMENDATION / FINDINGS AND REPORTS SUBMITTED	BOARD DECISION	OUTCOME
				(c) community participation; (d) cross-country participation in supervision missions; (e) Panel of Scientists; (f) possible repeat pilot
#20 Ecuador / Mining Development and Environmental Control Technical Assistance Project	Yes 12/99	**Investigation** **Eligibility Report 4/00** The Panel found the Request met the eligibility criteria **Panel Findings** **Investigation Report 2/01** The Panel concluded that Management was substantially in compliance with the provisions of OD 4.01 on Environmental Assessment (formerly OD 4.00, Annex A), OPN 11.02 on Wildlands (now OP/BP 4.04 on Natural Habitats), and OD 13.05 on Project Supervision. Management was found in apparent violation of certain provisions of the policies and procedures on Environmental Assessment (OD 4.00, Annex A, and OD 4.01) relating to processing, geographical scope, baseline data, and concerning consultation during preparation	**Approved (5/00)** The Board approved the Panel's recommendation on a non-objection basis The Board approved Management's recommendations on a non-objection basis on April 18, 2001	Management accepted Panel findings and proposed the following actions and next steps: (a) monitoring; (b) enforcement of license agreements; (c) additional publications and workshops; (d) development of consultation mechanisms; (e) support for conservation and environmental management in Ecuador; (f) strengthening of environmental institutions. No remedial efforts were proposed with regard to the claims made by the Requesters
#21 India / NTPC Power Generation Project (2nd Request)	No 12/99	The Request was not registered because the loan was closed in March 1999		
#22 Chad / Petroleum Development and Pipeline; Management of Petroleum Economy; and Petroleum Sector Management Capacity Building Projects	Yes 4/01	Processing of the Request delated due to electoral and post-election process. The Panel's Eligibility Report due by September 17. 2001.		
#23 India Coal Sector Environmental and Social Mitigation Project; Coal Sector Rehabilitation Project	Yes 6/01	Pending Eligibility Report due August 20, 2001		

25

TABLE 3
Alleged Violations of Policies and Procedures

REQUEST	VIOLATIONS CLAIMED BY REQUESTERS
#1 Nepal / Arun III Proposed Hydroelectric Project and Restructuring of IDA Credit	Economic Evaluation of Investment Operations (OP/ BP 10.04) Disclosure of Operational Information, (BP 17.50), Outline for a Project Information Document (PID) (BP 10.00, Annex A), Environmental Assessment (OD 4.01), Involuntary Resettlement (OD 4.30), Indigenous Peoples (OD 4.20)
#2 Ethiopia / Exportation	Dispute over Defaults on External Debt, Expropriation and Breach of Contract (OMS 1.28), Disclosure of Operational Information (BP 17.50)
#3 Tanzania Emergency Power Project	Article V Section 1(c), IDA Articles of Agreement, Article V Section 1(d), IDA Articles of Agreement, Article V Section 1(g), IDA Articles of Agreement, Environmental Aspects of Bank Work (OMS NO. 236), Environmental Assessment (OD 4.01)
#4 Brazil / Rondônia Natural Resources Management Project	Project Supervision (OD 13.05), Forestry Policy (OP 4.36), Wildlands Policy (OP 11.02), Indigenous Peoples (OD 4.20), Involvement of NGOs in Bank-supported Activities (OD 14.70), Project Monitoring and Evaluation (OD 10.70), Investment Lending: Identification to Board Presentation (BP 10.00), Suspension of Disbursements (OD 13.40)
#6 Bangladesh / Jamuna Bridge Project	Environmental Assessment (OD 4.01 and Annexes), Involuntary Resettlement (OD 4.30), Involvement of NGOs in Bank-supported Activities (OD 14.70)
#7 Argentina / Paraguay: Yacyretá Hydroelectric Project	Environmental Policy for Dam and Reservoir Projects (OD 4.00 - ANNEX B), Environmental Assessment (OD 4.01), Indigenous Peoples (OD 4.20), Involuntary Resettlement (OD 4.30), Project Monitoring and Evaluation (OD 10.70), Project Supervision (OD 13.05), Wildlands (OPN 11.02), Cultural Property (OPN 11.03), Environmental Aspects of Bank Work (OMS 2.36), Suspension of Disbursements (OD 13.40)
#8 Bangladesh / Jute Sector Adjustment Credit	Environmental Policy for Dam and Reservoir Projects (OD 4.00 - ANNEX B), Environmental Assessment (OD 4.01) Indigenous Peoples (OD 4.20), Involuntary Resettlement (OD 4.30)
#9 Brazil / Itaparica Resettlement and Irrigation Project	Environmental Policy for Dam and Reservoir Projects (OD 4.00 - ANNEX B), Environmental Assessment (OD4.01) Involuntary Resettlement (OD 4.30), Indigenous Peoples (OD 4.20), Project Supervision (OD 13.05)
#10 India / NTPC Power Generation Project	Economic Evaluation of Investment Operations (OP/BP 10.04), Environmental Assessment (OD 4.01), Involuntary Resettlement (OD 4.30), Indigenous Peoples (OD 4.20), Project Supervision (OD 13.05)
#11 India / Ecodevelopment Project	Indigenous Peoples (OD 4.20), Involuntary Resettlement (OD 4.30), Forestry (OP 4.36)
#12 Lesotho / South Africa Phase 1B of Lesotho Highlands Water Project	Environmental Policy for Dam and Reservoir Project (OD 4.00), Economic Evaluation of Investment Options (OD 10.04) Poverty Reduction (OD 4.15), Water Resources and Management (OP 4.07)
#13 Nigeria / Lagos Drainage and Sanitation Project	Involuntary Resettlement (OD 4.30), Poverty Reduction (OD 4.15), Gender Dimensions of Development (OD 4.20), Project Monitoring and Evaluation (OD 10.70), Economic Evaluation of Investment Operations (OP/BP 10.04), Article V Section 1(g) Articles of Agreement
#14 Brazil / Land Reform Poverty Alleviation Project	Poverty Reduction (OD 4.15), Involvement of NGOs in Bank Operations (GP 14.70), Disclosure of Operational Information (BP 17.50)
#15 Lesotho / Highlands Water Project from Swissborough Diamond Mines Ltd. & Others	Disclosure of Information (BP 17.50), Disputes over Defaults on External Debt, Expropriation and Breach of Contract (BP 7.40)
#16 China / Western Poverty Reduction Project	Disclosure of Information (BP 17.50), Involuntary Resettlement (OD 4.30), Environmental Assessment (OD 4.01), Indigenous Peoples (OD 4.20), Pest Management (OP 4.09)

OPERATIONS

TABLE 3
Alleged Violations of Policies and Procedures, continued

REQUEST	VIOLATIONS CLAIMED BY REQUESTERS
#17 Argentina / Special Structural Adjustment Loan	Project Supervision (OD 13.05), Poverty Reduction (OD 4.15), Project Monitoring and Evaluation (OP/BP 10.70), Suspension of Disbursements (OP/BP 13.40), Disclosure of Operational Information (BP 17.50)
#18 Brazil / Land Reform Poverty Alleviation Project (2nd Request)	Poverty Reduction (OD 4.15), Disclosure of Operational Information (BP 17.50), Project Supervision (13.05)
#19 Kenya / Lake Victoria Environmental Management Project	Environmental Assessment (OD 4.01), Poverty Alleviation (OD 4.15), Economic Evaluation of Investment Projects (OP 10.04) Project Supervision (OD 13.05)
#20 Ecuador / Mining Development and Environmental Control Technical Assistance Project	Environmental Assessment (OD 4.01), Wildlands (OPN 11.02), Indigenous Peoples (OD 4.20), Project Supervision (OD 13.05)
#21 India / NTPC Power Generation Project	Involuntary Resettlement (OD 4.30), Project Supervision (OD 13.05)
#22 Chad / Petroleum Development and Pipeline Project; Management of Petroleum Economy Project; and Petroleum Sector Management Capacity Building Project	Environmental Assessment (OD 4.01), Natural Habitats (OP/BP 4.04), Pest Management (OP 4.09), Poverty Reduction (OD 4.15), Indigenous Peoples (OD 4.20), Forestry (OP 4.36), Disclosure of Operational Information (BP 17.50), Economic Evaluation of Investment Operations (OP 10.04), Management of Cultural Property in Bank-Financed Projects (OPN 11.03), Project Supervision (OD 13.05)
#23 India Coal Sector Environmental and Social Mitigation Project and Coal Sector Rehabilitation Project	Environmental Assessment (OD 4.01), Indigenous Peoples (OD 4.20), Involuntary Resettlement (OD 4.30), Disclosure of Operational Information (BP 17.50), Management of Cultural Property in Bank-Financed Projects (OPN 11.03), Project Supervision (OD 13.05)

**Figure 3
Percentage of Requests Received by Region, 1994 - 2001**

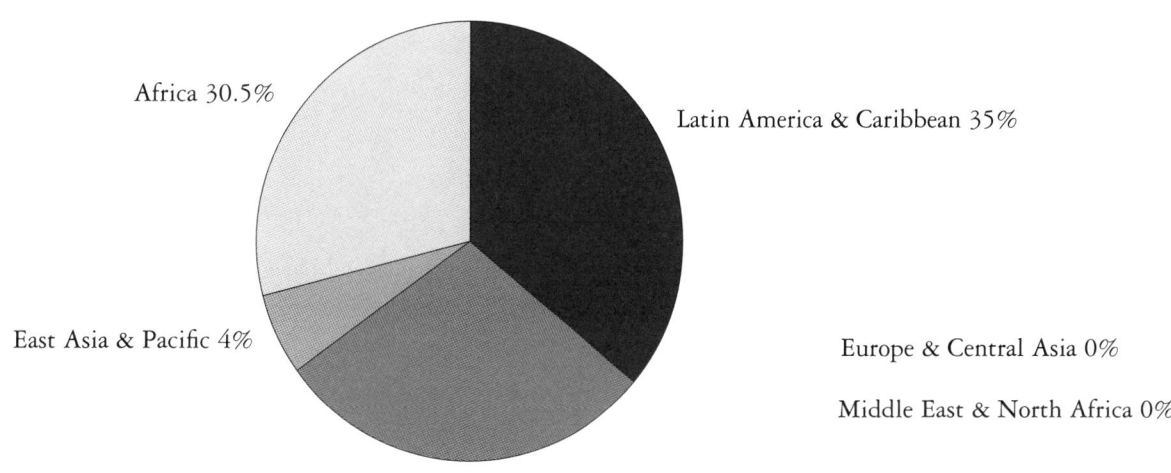

Africa 30.5%
Latin America & Caribbean 35%
East Asia & Pacific 4%
Europe & Central Asia 0%
Middle East & North Africa 0%
South Asia 30.5%

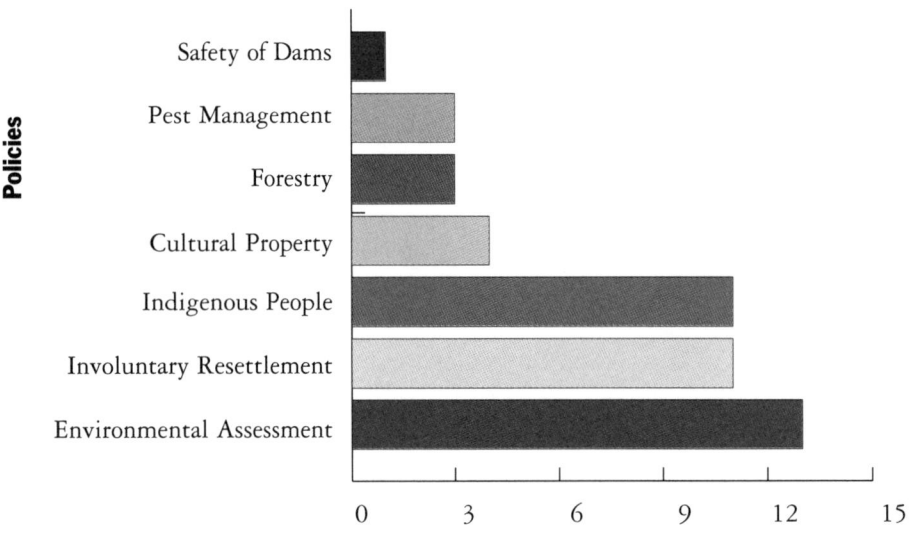

**Figure 4
Times Requesters Claimed Violation of Safeguard Policies
August 1994 to July 2001**

Outreach and Disclosure

The Inspection Panel continued its internal and external outreach campaign during this period in an effort to make its existence, role, and functions better known by all stakeholders within and outside the World Bank. Internally, the Panel Members and staff of the Secretariat met with several Bank Regional Management Teams to discuss the role of the Panel and the procedures to be followed after a Request for Inspection is filed. As part of its continued campaign to reach as large a number of stakeholders as possible, the Panel is in the process of redesigning its website.

The Panel received a number of invitations to participate in meetings and seminars related to the Panel's role as an accountability mechanism available to people that could be adversely affected by Bank-financed projects. These events included the European Investment Bank "Roundtable on Information and Transparency," in Brussels in October 2000; a conference on "Cooperação Técnica e Financeira, Bancos e Meio Ambiente," in São Paulo; the International Environmental Lawyers Annual Meeting, in Oregon; the Asian Development Bank Annual Meetings, in Hawaii, and the CCAT Conference in Quebec.

Disclosure

The rules for disclosure of documents generated by the Inspection Panel process are stipulated in the Resolution establishing the Panel as well as in the 1996 and 1999 Clarifications the Executive Directors adopted.

In the 1996 Clarifications the Executive Directors instructed Management "to make significant efforts to make the Inspection Panel better known in borrowing countries...." In the 1999 Clarifications, the Board underscored the need for Management to make significant efforts to make the Panel better known, and emphasized the importance of prompt disclosure of information to claimants and the public. The Board also required that "such information be provided by Management to claimants in their language, to the extent possible."

The Panel has made every effort to keep its processes open and transparent—consistent with the public disclosure policy adopted by the Bank's Board in 1993. The Inspection Panel's website continually updates the status of Panel activities, and continues to receive a large number of queries.

The Panel Register

In an effort to deal transparently with Requests, the Panel has maintained a Register. The Executive Secretary records the dates and all actions taken in connection with the processing of a Request, as well as the dates on which any formal notification is sent or received. The Panel keeps the Requester informed about the process. This Register is open to the public, and is also posted on the Panel's website to ensure wider disclosure.

A notice that a Request has been registered, and all other notices or documents issued by the Panel, are made available to the public at: (a) the Bank's InfoShop in Washington, D.C.; (b) the Bank's Resident Mission, Regional or Country Office for the country where the project relating to the Request is located, or at the relevant regional office; (c) the Bank's Paris and Tokyo offices; and (d) the Panel's website: *www.inspectionpanel.org*.

When permitted by the Resolution, the Bank makes documents relating to each Request available to the public. Under Paragraph 25 of the Resolution, Requests for Inspection, Panel Recommendations, and Board decisions are to be made available to the public after the Executive Directors have considered a Panel Recommendation on, or the results of, an investigation. During the 1996 review by the Board, the Directors clarified that provision to ensure that Management Responses would also be made available within three days after action by the Board, along with the documents already cited. The Board also said that Management should make available any legal opinions issued by the Bank Legal Department related to Inspection Panel matters promptly after Board action, unless the Board decides otherwise in a specific case.

World Bank Annual Meetings

The Panel has participated in each Annual Meeting of the World Bank since 1994. Participation in the Meetings has allowed the Panel opportunities to meet with Government officials, private sector organizations and citizens, and numerous NGOs. The experience has been invaluable to the Panel. When the Annual Meeting is held outside the United States, it has been particularly useful to the Panel in making organizations from that region more aware of the Panel's work, the extent of its mandate, and the procedures for requesting an inspection.

Public Inquiries

Given the unprecedented nature of the Panel mechanism in an international organization, there continues to be a substantial demand for general information about the Panel and its activities from the press, NGOs and other organizations, academics, Bank staff, and others. The availability of *The Inspection Panel* brochure in several languages responds to the needs of many such public inquiries.

First Review of the Inspection Panel Mechanism

The Resolution establishing the Panel called for a review of the experience of the inspection function after two years from the date of the appointment of the first members of the Panel. The Board completed its review of the Inspection Panel in October 1996. This resulted in the *1996 Clarification of Certain Aspects of the Resolution*. This first review focused on four main areas: preliminary assessment, eligibility and access, outreach, and the role of the Board.

The Panel was instructed that it could undertake a "preliminary assessment" of the damages alleged by the Requester, if it believed that it would be appropriate, and in particular when such assessment could lead to a resolution of the matter without need of a full investigation. The preliminary stage was not to be used to establish that a serious violation of the Bank's policy had actually resulted in damages suffered by the affected party, but rather to establish whether the complaint, on the surface, was justified and warranted a full investigation.

In terms of eligibility and access, the "affected party" described in the Resolution as "a community of persons such as an organization, association, society or other grouping of individuals" was defined to include any two or more persons who share common interests or concerns. The Review endorsed the understanding that the Panel's mandate is limited to cases of alleged failure by the Bank to follow its operational policies and procedures with respect to the design, appraisal, or implementation of projects, including cases of alleged failure by the Bank to follow up on the borrowers' obligations under loan agreements, with respect to such polices and procedures. Specific procurement decisions, however, whether made by the Bank or a borrower, could not be subject to Panel inspection.

On outreach, Management was instructed to make its response to Requests available to the public within three days after the Board decides whether to authorize an inspection. It must also make publicly available the opinions of the General Counsel related to Inspection Panel matters promptly after the Executive Directors have dealt with the issues involved. Management was also instructed to make significant efforts to make the Panel better known in borrowing countries.

With regard to the role of the Board, the Clarifications reaffirmed the Board's authority to interpret the Resolution and authorize inspections. In applying the Resolution to specific cases, the Board confirmed that the Panel will apply the Resolution as it understands it, subject to the Board's review.

Second Review of the Inspection Panel Mechanism

In September 1997, the Board concluded they should again review the functioning of the Inspection Panel. In February 1998, after considering proposals by the Senior Vice President and General Counsel as well as the Inspection Panel's related comments, the Board decided to create a Working Group, composed of three Part I and three Part II Executive Directors. The Working Group would review the operations of the Inspection Panel and propose solutions primarily aimed at achieving greater Board unity in cases where the Panel had recommended an investigation. The Working Group subsequently proposed several clarifications to the Resolution. On April 20, 1999, acting on the proposal by the Working Group, the Board of Executive Directors issued *Conclusions of the Board's Second Review of the Inspection Panel* which reaffirmed "the Resolution, the importance of the Panel's function, its independence and integrity."

The second review provided clarification on the application of the Resolution in four principal areas: preliminary assessment, Board authorization of an investigation, material adverse effect, and action plans.

The Board determined that the "preliminary assessment" concept in the eligibility stage of the request for inspection process, as provided for in the 1996 Clarifications, was no longer needed.

Board authorization, if the Panel so recommended, would be authorized without the Board making any judgment on the merits of the Request. Authorization would be based solely on the technical "eligibility criteria" of the Request.

In its investigation report the Panel was directed to discuss only those material adverse effects, alleged in the Request, that had totally or partially resulted from serious Bank failure of compliance with its policies and procedures. If the Request alleged a material adverse effect and the Panel found that it was not totally or partially caused by Bank failure, the Panel's report would so state without entering into an analysis of the material adverse effect or its causes.

The Board decided that "Action Plans" agreed between the borrower and the Bank in consultation with the Requesters, that seek to improve project implementation are outside the Panel's mandate. The Board noted that in the event of agreement by the Bank and borrower on an action plan for the project, Management will communicate to the Panel the nature and outcomes of consultations with affected parties on the action plan. Such an action plan, if warranted, will normally be considered by the Board in conjunction with the Management's report, submitted after an investigation. The Panel may submit to the Executive Directors for their consideration a report on their view of the adequacy of consultations with affected parties in the preparation of action plans. The Board should not ask the Panel for its view on other aspects of the action plans nor would it ask the Panel to monitor the implementation of the action plans. The Panel's view on consultation with affected parties will be based on the information available to it by all means, but additional country visits will take place only by government invitation.

Assessment of Actions Plans by the Panel was limited to the Panel's view on the adequacy of consultations with affected parities in preparation of the plans. The Board would not ask the Panel for its views on other aspects of Action Plans, nor would it ask the Panel to monitor the implementation of Action Plans.

As in the 1996 Clarifications, the Board underlined the need for Management to make significant efforts to make the Panel better known in borrowing countries and emphasized the importance of prompt disclosure of information to claimants and the public by Management, and that to the extent possible, such information should be provided to claimants in their language.

Sources of Further Information

The Inspection Panel's website *www.inspectionpanel.org* provides:
- Current information on Panel cases and activities
- Each step in the processing of Requests
- Panel Reports
- Panel *Operating Procedures*, the IBRD/IDA Resolution establishing the Panel, and the 1996 and 1999 Clarifications to the Resolution.

World Bank InfoShop
701 18th Street, NW, Washington, D.C. 20433
Tel: (202) 473-2941; Fax: (202) 477-0604
Website: *www.worldbank.org/infoshop*

World Bank Public Information Centers
PARIS
66 avenue d'Iéna, 75116 Paris, France
Tel: (33-1) 40 69 30 26; Fax: (33-1) 40 69 30 69
Email: pparis@worldbank.org

TOKYO
10th Floor Fukoku-Seimei Building, #2-2-2 Uchisaiwai-cho,
Chiyoda-ku, Tokyo 100, Japan
Tel: (813) 3597-6676; Fax: (813) 3597-6695
Email: ptokyo@worldbank.org

Bank Resident Missions, Regional or Country Office
Where the project relating to a Request is located.

All Requests for Inspection should be sent directly to:
The Inspection Panel
1818 H Street, MC10-1007
Washington, D.C. 20433.
Email: Ipanel@worldbank.org

Any World Bank office around the world can be asked to forward a Request, unopened, to the Inspection Panel.

Administration and Budget

The Resolution provides that the "Panel shall be given such budgetary resources as shall be sufficient to carry out its activities."

The administrative arrangements for the Panel provide for the Chairman to work on a full-time basis supported by a small Secretariat. He calls on the two part-time Panel members on a case-by-case basis as required by the Panel's workload related to Requests, public inquiries, and consultations as well as institutional and administrative matters. In practice the Panel has worked by consensus with the two part-time members fully involved in all activities related to Requests, and informational, institutional, and administrative matters. The Resolution provides that if the workload reaches a level that would make it reasonable for the Panel to recommend it, the Board would appoint one or both part-time members on a full-time basis. The Panel has not yet recommended this, even though the workload of the Panel has progressively increased during each year of its existence.

The demand-driven nature of the Panel's work requires a flexible budgetary strategy to ensure that sufficient resources are available to process all Requests received. Annex 5 contains a breakdown of the Panel's budget and expenditures for fiscal 2001.

Annex 1

Resolution No. IBRD 93-10
Resolution No. IDA 93-6
"The World Bank Inspection Panel"

September 22, 1993

INTERNATIONAL BANK FOR RECONSTRUCTION AND DEVELOPMENT
INTERNATIONAL DEVELOPMENT ASSOCIATION

Resolution No. IBRD 93-10

Resolution No. IDA 93-6

"The World Bank Inspection Panel"

The Executive Directors:
Hereby resolve:

1. There is established an independent Inspection Panel (hereinafter called the Panel), which shall have the powers and shall function as stated in this resolution.

Composition of the Panel

2. The Panel shall consist of three members of different nationalities from Bank member countries. The President, after consultation with the Executive Directors, shall nominate the members of the Panel to be appointed by the Executive Directors.

3. The first members of the Panel shall be appointed as follows: one for three years, one for four years and one for five years. Each vacancy thereafter shall be filled for a period of five years, provided that no member may serve for more than one term. The term of appointment of each member of the Panel shall be subject to the continuity of the inspection function established by this Resolution.

4. Members of the Panel shall be selected on the basis of their ability to deal thoroughly and fairly with the requests brought to them, their integrity and their independence from the Bank's Management, and their exposure to developmental issues and to living conditions in developing countries. Knowledge and experience of the Bank's operations will also be desirable.

5. Executive Directors, Alternates, Advisors and staff members of the Bank Group may not serve on the Panel until two years have elapsed since the end of their service in the Bank Group. For purposes of this Resolution, the term "staff" shall mean all persons holding Bank Group appointments as defined in Staff Rule 4.01 including persons holding consultant and local consultant appointments.

6. A Panel member shall be disqualified from participation in the hearing and investigation of any request related to a matter in which he/she has a personal interest or had significant involvement in any capacity.

7. The Panel member initially appointed for five years shall be the first Chairperson of the Panel, and shall hold such office for one year. Thereafter, the members of the Panel shall elect a Chairperson for a period of one year.

8. Members of the Panel may be removed from office only by decision of the Executive Directors, for cause.

9. With the exception of the Chairperson who shall work on a full-time basis at Bank headquarters, members of the Panel shall be expected to work on a full-time basis only when their workload justifies such an arrangement, as will be decided by the Executive Directors on the recommendation of the Panel.

10. In the performance of their functions, members of the Panel shall be officials of the Bank enjoying the privileges and immunities accorded to Bank officials, and shall be subject to the requirements of the Bank's Articles of Agreement concerning their exclusive loyalty to the Bank and to the obligations of subparagraphs (c) and (d) of paragraph 3.1 and paragraph 3.2 of the Principles of Staff Employment concerning their conduct as officials of the Bank. Once they begin to work on a full-time basis, they shall receive remuneration at a level to be determined by the Executive Directors upon a recommendation of the President, plus normal benefits available to Bank fixed-term staff. Prior to that time, they shall be remunerated on a *per diem* basis and shall be reimbursed for their expenses on the same basis as the members of the Bank's Administrative Tribunal. Members of the Panel may not be employed by the Bank Group, following the end of their service on the Panel.

11. The President, after consultation with the Executive Directors, shall assign a staff member to the Panel as Executive Secretary, who need not act on a full-time basis until the workload so justifies. The Panel shall be given such budgetary resources as shall be sufficient to carry out its activities.

Powers of the Panel

12. The Panel shall receive requests for inspection presented to it by an affected party in the territory of the borrower which is not a single individual (i.e., a community of persons such as an organization, association, society or other grouping of individuals), or by the local representative of such party or by another representative in the exceptional cases where the party submitting the request contends that appropriate representation is not locally available and the Executive Directors so agree at the time they consider the request for inspection. Any such representative shall present to the Panel written evidence that he is acting as agent of the party on behalf of which the request is made. The affected party must demonstrate that its rights or interests have been or are likely to be directly affected by an action or omission of the Bank as a result of a failure of the Bank to follow its operational policies and procedures with respect to the design, appraisal and/or implementation of a project financed by the Bank (including situations where the Bank is alleged to have failed in its follow-up on the borrower's obligations under loan agreements with respect to such policies and procedures) provided in all cases that such failure has had, or threatens to have, a material adverse effect. In view of the institutional responsibilities of Executive Directors in the observance by the Bank of its operational policies and procedures, an Executive Director may in special cases of serious alleged violations of such policies and procedures ask the Panel for an investigation, subject to the requirements of paragraphs 13 and 14 below. The Executive Directors, acting as a Board, may at any time instruct the Panel to conduct an investigation. For purposes of this Resolution, "operational policies and procedures" consist of the Bank's Operational Policies, Bank Procedures and Operational Directives, and similar documents issued before these series were started, and does not include Guidelines and Best Practices and similar documents or statements.

13. The Panel shall satisfy itself before a request for inspection is heard that the subject matter of the request has been dealt with by the Management of the Bank and Management has failed to demonstrate that it has followed, or is taking adequate steps to follow the Bank's policies and procedures. The Panel shall also satisfy itself that the alleged violation of the Bank's policies and procedures is of a serious character.

14. In considering requests under paragraph 12 above, the following requests shall not be heard by the Panel:

(a) Complaints with respect to actions which are the responsibility of other parties, such as a borrower, or potential borrower, and which do not involve any action or omission on the part of the Bank.

(b) Complaints against procurement decisions by Bank borrowers from suppliers of goods and services financed or expected to be financed by the Bank under a loan agreement, or from losing tenderers for the supply of any such goods and services, which will continue to be addressed by staff under existing procedures.

(c) Requests filed after the Closing Date of the loan financing the project with respect to which the request is filed or after the loan financing the project has been substantially disbursed.[1]

(d) Requests related to a particular matter or matters over which the Panel has already made its recommendation upon having received a prior request, unless justified by new evidence or circumstances not known at the time of the prior request.

15. The Panel shall seek the advice of the Bank's Legal Department on matters related to the Bank's rights and obligations with respect to the request under consideration.

Procedures

16. Requests for inspection shall be in writing and shall state all relevant facts, including, in the case of a request by an affected party, the harm suffered by or threatened to such party or parties by the alleged action or omission of the Bank. All requests shall explain the steps already taken to deal with the issue, as well as the nature of the alleged actions or omissions and shall specify the actions taken to bring the issue to the attention of Management, and Management's response to such action.

17. The Chairperson of the Panel shall inform the Executive Directors and the President of the Bank promptly upon receiving a request for inspection.

18. Within 21 days of being notified of a request for inspection, the Management of the Bank shall provide the Panel with evidence that it has complied, or intends to comply with the Bank's relevant policies and procedures.

19. Within 21 days of receiving the response of the Management as provided in the preceding paragraph, the Panel shall determine whether the request meets the eligibility criteria set out in paragraphs 12 to 14 above and shall make a recommendation to the Executive Directors as to whether the matter should be investigated. The recommendation of the Panel shall be circulated to the Executive Directors for decision within the normal distribution period. In case the request was initiated by an affected party, such party shall be informed of the decision of the Executive Directors within two weeks of the date of such decision.

20. If a decision is made by the Executive Directors to investigate the request, the Chairperson of the Panel shall designate one or more of the Panel's members (Inspectors) who shall have primary responsibility for conducting the

---

[1] This will be deemed to be the case when at least 95 percent of the loan proceeds have been disbursed.

inspection. The Inspector(s) shall report his/her (their) findings to the Panel within a period to be determined by the Panel taking into account the nature of each request.

21. In the discharge of their functions, the members of the Panel shall have access to all staff who may contribute information and to all pertinent Bank records and shall consult as needed with the Director General, Operations Evaluation Department and the Internal Auditor. The borrower and the Executive Director representing the borrowing (or guaranteeing) country shall be consulted on the subject matter both before the Panel's recommendation on whether to proceed with the investigation and during the investigation. Inspection in the territory of such country shall be carried out with its prior consent.

22. The Panel shall submit its report to the Executive Directors and the President. The report of the Panel shall consider all relevant facts, and shall conclude with the Panel's findings on whether the Bank has complied with all relevant Bank policies and procedures.

23. Within six weeks from receiving the Panel's findings, Management will submit to the Executive Directors for their consideration a report indicating its recommendations in response to such findings. The findings of the Panel and the actions completed during project preparation also will be discussed in the Staff Appraisal Report when the project is submitted to the Executive Directors for financing. In all cases of a request made by an affected party, the Bank shall, within two weeks of the Executive Directors' consideration of the matter, inform such party of the results of the investigation and the action taken in its respect, if any.

Decisions of the Panel

24. All decisions of the Panel on procedural matters, its recommendations to the Executive Directors on whether to proceed with the investigation of a request, and its reports pursuant to paragraph 22, shall be reached by consensus and, in the absence of a consensus, the majority and minority views shall be stated.

Reports

25. After the Executive Directors have considered a request for an inspection as set out in paragraph 19, the Bank shall make such request publicly available together with the recommendation of the Panel on whether to proceed with the inspection and the decision of the Executive Directors in this respect. The Bank shall make publicly available the report submitted by the Panel pursuant to paragraph 22 and the Bank's response thereon within two weeks after consideration by the Executive Directors of the report.

26. In addition to the material referred to in paragraph 25, the Panel shall furnish an annual report to the President and the Executive Directors concerning its activities. The annual report shall be published by the Bank.

Review

27. The Executive Directors shall review the experience of the inspection function established by this Resolution after two years from the date of the appointment of the first members of the Panel.

Application to IDA projects

28. In this resolution, references to the Bank and to loans include references to the Association and to development credits.

Annex 2

1996 Clarification of Certain Aspects of the Resolution

REVIEW OF THE RESOLUTION ESTABLISHING THE INSPECTION PANEL
1996 CLARIFICATION OF CERTAIN ASPECTS OF THE RESOLUTION

The Resolution establishing the Inspection Panel calls for a review after two years from the date of appointment of the first panel members. On October 17, 1996, the Executive Directors of the Bank and IDA completed the review process (except for the question of inspection of World Bank Group private sector projects) by considering and endorsing the clarifications recommended by Management on the basis of the discussions of the Executive Directors' Committee on Development Effectiveness (CODE). The Inspection Panel and Management are requested by the Executive Directors to observe the clarifications in their application of the Resolution. The clarifications are set out below.

The Panel's Function

Since the Resolution limits the first phase of the inspection process to ascertaining the eligibility of the request, this phase should normally be completed within the 21 days stated in the Resolution. However, in cases where the Inspection Panel believes that it would be appropriate to undertake a "preliminary assessment" of the damages alleged by the requester (in particular when such preliminary assessment could lead to a resolution of the matter without the need for a full investigation), the Panel may undertake the preliminary assessment and indicate to the Board the date on which it would present its findings and recommendations as to the need, if any, for a full investigation. If such a date is expected by the Panel to exceed eight weeks from the date of receipt of Management's comments, the Panel should seek Board approval for the extension, possibly on a "no-objection" basis. What is needed at this preliminary stage is not to establish that a serious violation of the Bank's policy has actually resulted in damages suffered by the affected party, but rather to establish whether the complaint is prima facie justified and warrants a full investigation because it is eligible under the Resolution. Panel investigations will continue to result in "findings" and the Board will continue to act on investigations on the basis of recommendations of Management with respect to such remedial action as may be needed.

Eligibility and Access

It is understood that the "affected party" which the Resolution describes as "a community of persons such as an organization, association, society or other grouping of individuals" includes any two or more persons who share some common interests or concerns. The word "project" as used in the Resolution has the same meaning as it generally has in the Bank's practice, and includes projects under consideration by Bank management as well as projects already approved by the Executive Directors.

The Panel's mandate does not extend to reviewing the consistency of the Bank's practice with *any* of its policies and procedures, but, as stated in the Resolution, is limited to cases of alleged failure by the Bank to follow its operational policies and procedures *with respect to the design, appraisal and/or implementation of projects*, including cases of alleged failure by the bank to follow-up on the borrowers' obligations under loan agreements, with respect to such policies and procedures.

No procurement action is subject to inspection by the Panel, whether taken by the Bank or by a borrower. A separate mechanism is available for addressing procurement-related complaints.

Outreach

Management will make its response to requests for inspection available to the public within three days after the Board has decided on whether to authorize the inspection. Management will also make available to the public opinions of the General Counsel related to Inspection Panel matters promptly after the Executive Directors have dealt with the issues involved, unless the Board decides otherwise in a specific case.

Management will make significant efforts to make the Inspection Panel better known in borrowing countries, but will not provide technical assistance or funding to potential requesters.

Composition of the Panel

No change in the composition of the Panel is being made at this time.

Role of the Board

The Board will continue to have authority to (i) interpret the Resolution; and (ii) authorize inspections. In applying the Resolution to specific cases, the Panel will apply it as it understands it, subject to the Board's review. As stated in the Resolution, "[t]he Panel shall seek the advice of the Bank's Legal Department on matters related to the Bank's rights and obligations with respect to the request under consideration."

October 17, 1996

Annex 3

1999 Clarification of the Board's Second Review of the Inspection Panel

1999 Conclusions of the Board's Second Review of the Inspection Panel

The Executive Directors approved today, April 20, 1999, with immediate effect, the report of the Working Group on the Second Review of the Inspection Panel, as revised in light of the extensive consultations that took place after the report was first circulated.

The report confirms the soundness of the Resolution establishing the Inspection Panel (IBRD Resolution No. 93-10, IDA Resolution No. 93-6 of September 22, 1993, hereinafter "the Resolution") and provides clarifications for its application. These clarifications supplement the clarifications issued by the Board on October 17, 1996 and prevail over them in case of conflict. The report's recommendations approved by the Board are as follows:

1. The Board reaffirms the Resolution, the importance of the Panel's function, its independence and integrity.

2. Management will follow the Resolution. It will not communicate with the Board on matters associated with the request for inspection, except as provided for in the Resolution. It will thus direct its response to the request, including any steps it intends to take to address its failures, if any, to the Panel. Management will report to the Board any recommendations it may have, after the Panel completes its inspection and submits its findings, as envisaged in paragraph 23 of the Resolution.

3. In its initial response to the request for inspection, Management will provide evidence that

   i. it has complied with the relevant Bank operational policies and procedures; or that

   ii. there are serious failures attributable exclusively to its own actions or omissions in complying, but that it intends to comply with the relevant policies and procedures; or that

   iii. the serious failures that may exist are exclusively attributable to the borrower or to other factors external to the Bank; or that

   iv. the serious failures that may exist are attributable both to the Bank's non-compliance with the relevant operational policies and procedures and to the borrower or other external factors.

The Inspection Panel may independently agree or disagree, totally or partially, with Management's position and will proceed accordingly.

4. When Management responds, admitting serious failures that are attributable exclusively or partly to the Bank, it will provide evidence that it has complied or intends to comply with the relevant operating policies and procedures. This response will contain only those actions that the Bank has implemented or can implement by itself.

5. The Inspection Panel will satisfy itself as to whether the Bank's compliance or evidence of intention to comply is adequate, and reflect this assessment in its reporting to the Board.

6. The Panel will determine the eligibility of a request for inspection independently of any views that may be expressed by Management. With respect to matters relating to the Bank's rights and obligations with respect to the request under consideration, the Panel will seek the advice of the Bank's Legal Department as required by the Resolution.

7. For its recommendation on whether an investigation should be carried out, the Panel will satisfy itself that all the eligibility criteria provided for in the Resolution have been met. It will base its recommendation on the information presented in the request, in the Management response, and on other documentary evidence. The Panel may decide to visit the project country if it believes that this is necessary to establish the eligibility of the request. In respect of such field visits, the Panel will not report on the Bank's failure to comply with its policies and procedures or its resulting material adverse effect; any definitive assessment of a serious failure of the Bank that has caused material adverse effect will be done after the Panel has completed its investigation.

8. The original time limit, set forth in the Resolution for both Management's response to the request and the Panel's recommendation, will be strictly observed except for reasons of force majeure, i.e. reasons that are clearly beyond Management's or the Panel's control, respectively, as may be approved by the Board on a no objection basis.

9. If the Panel so recommends, the Board will authorize an investigation without making a judgment on the merits of the claimants' request, and without discussion except with respect to the following technical eligibility criteria:

a. The affected party consists of any two or more persons with common interests or concerns and who are in the borrower's territory (Resolution para.12).

b. The request does assert in substance that a serious violation by the Bank of its operational policies and procedures has or is likely to have a material adverse effect on the requester (Resolution paras. 12 and 14a).

c. The request does assert that its subject matter has been brought to Management's attention and that, in the requester's view, Management has failed to respond adequately demonstrating that it has followed or is taking steps to follow the Bank's policies and procedures (Resolution para. 13).

d. The matter is not related to procurement (Resolution para. 14b).

e. The related loan has not been closed or substantially disbursed (Resolution para. 14c).

f. The Panel has not previously made a recommendation on the subject matter or, if it has, that the request does assert that there is new evidence or circumstances not known at the time of the prior request (Resolution para. 14d).

10. Issues of interpretation of the Resolution will be cleared with the Board.

11. The "preliminary assessment" concept, as described in the October 1996 Clarification, is no longer needed. The paragraph entitled "The Panel's Function" in the October 1996 "Clarifications" is thus deleted.

12. The profile of Panel activities, in-country, during the course of an investigation, should be kept as low as possible in keeping with its role as a fact-finding body on behalf of the Board. The Panel's methods of investigation should not create the impression that it is investigating the borrower's performance. However, the Board, acknowledging the important role of the Panel in contacting the requesters and in fact-finding on behalf of the Board, welcomes the Panel's efforts to gather information through consultations with affected people. Given the need to conduct such work in an independent

and low-profile manner, the Panel – and Management – should decline media contacts while an investigation is pending or underway. Under those circumstances in which, in the judgment of the Panel or Management, it is necessary to respond to the media, comments should be limited to the process. They will make it clear that the Panel's role is to investigate the Bank and not the borrower.

13. As required by the Resolution, the Panel's report to the Board will focus on whether there is a serious Bank failure to observe its operational policies and procedures with respect to project design, appraisal and/or implementation. The report will include all relevant facts that are needed to understand fully the context and basis for the panel's findings and conclusions. The Panel will discuss in its written report only those material adverse effects, alleged in the request, that have totally or partially resulted from serious Bank failure of compliance with its policies and procedures. If the request alleges a material adverse effect and the Panel finds that it is not totally or partially caused by Bank failure, the Panel's report will so state without entering into analysis of the material adverse effect itself or its causes.

14. For assessing material adverse effect, the without-project situation should be used as the base case for comparison, taking into account what baseline information may be available. Non-accomplishments and unfulfilled expectations that do not generate a material deterioration compared to the without-project situation will not be considered as a material adverse effect for this purpose. As the assessment of material adverse effect in the context of the complex reality of a specific project can be difficult, the Panel will have to exercise carefully its judgment on these matters, and be guided by Bank policies and procedures where relevant.

15. A distinction has to be made between Management's report to the Board (Resolution para. 23), which addresses Bank failure and possible Bank remedial efforts and "action plans," agreed between the borrower and the Bank, in consultation with the requesters, that seek to improve project implementation. The latter "action plans" are outside the purview of the Resolution, its 1996 clarification, and these clarifications. In the event of agreement by the Bank and borrower on an action plan for the project, Management will communicate to the Panel the nature and outcomes of consultations with affected parties on the action plan. Such an action plan, if warranted, will normally be considered by the Board in conjunction with the Management's report, submitted under Resolution para. 23.

16. The Panel may submit to the Executive Directors for their consideration a report on their view of the adequacy of consultations with affected parties in the preparation of the action plans. The Board should not ask the Panel for its view on other aspects of the action plans nor would it ask the Panel to monitor the implementation of the action plans. The Panel's view on consultation with affected parties will be based on the information available to it by all means, but additional country visits will take place only by government invitation.

17. The Board underlines the need for Management to make significant efforts to make the Inspection Panel better known in borrowing countries, as specified in the 1996 "Clarifications."

18. The Board emphasizes the importance of prompt disclosure of information to claimants and the public, as stipulated in the Resolution (paras. 23 and 25) and in its 1996 Clarifications. The Board requires that such information be provided by Management to claimants in their language, to the extent possible.

19. The Board recognizes that enhancing the effectiveness of the Inspection Panel process through the above clarifications assumes adherence to them by all parties in good faith. It also assumes the borrowers' consent for field visits envisaged in the Resolution. If these assumptions prove to be incorrect, the Board will revisit the above conclusions.

Annex 4

Operating Procedures

> The Panel is currently in the process of revising its *Operating Procedures* to reflect the 1996 and 1999 Clarifications to the Resolution that established the Panel, as well as lessons learned and comments received during the first seven years of operation.

Contents

Operating Procedures
as adopted by the Panel on August 19, 1994

CONTENTS

Introduction — 50
    Composition — 50
    Purpose — 50
    Functions — 50
    Participants — 50
    Administration — 51

Subject Matter of Requests — 51
    Scope — 51
    Limitations — 51

Preparation of a Request — 52
    A. Who Can File a Request — 52
    B. Contents of a Request — 52
    C. Form of a Request — 52
        Written — 52
        Format — 53
        Language — 53
        Representatives — 53
        Documents — 53
    D. Delivery of Request — 53
    E. Advice on Preparation — 54

Procedures on Receipt of a Request — 54
    A. Register — 54
        Contents of Notice — 54
    B. Request Additional Information — 54
    C. Outside Scope — 54
        Records — 55
    D. Need for Review — 55
    E. Revised Request — 55

Management's Response — 55
    Clarification — 55

Panel Recommendation — 56

A. Basis	56
B. Required Criteria	56
Criteria for Satisfactory Response	56
Preliminary Review	57
Initial Study	57
C. Contents	57
D. Submission	57

Board Decision and Public Release

	58
Notification	58
Public Information	58

An Investigation

	58
A. Initial Procedures	58
B. Methods of Investigation	58
Consent Required	59
C. Participation of Requester	59
D. Participation of Third Parties	59

Panel Report

	59
Contents	59
Submission	60

Management's Recommendations

60

Board Decision and Public Release

60

General

	61
Business Days	61
Copies	61
Consultations	61
Access to Bank Staff and Information	61
Legal Advice	61
Confidentiality	61
Information to Requester and Public	61

Guidance on How to Prepare a Request for Inspection

	62
Model Form	63

INTRODUCTION

The Inspection Panel (the "Panel") is an independent forum established by the Executive Directors of the International Bank for Reconstruction and Development ("IBRD") and the International Development Association ("IDA") by IBRD Resolution No. 93-10 and the identical IDA Resolution No. 93-6 both adopted by the Executive Directors of the respective institutions on September 22, 1993 (collectively the "Resolution"). The text of the Resolution is in Annex 1. References in these procedures to the "Bank" includes the IBRD and IDA.

The Panel's authority is dictated by the Resolution: within that framework, these Operating Procedures are adopted by the Panel to provide detail to the operational provisions. The text is based on the Resolution and takes into account suggestions from outside sources.

In view of the unprecedented nature of the new inspection function the current procedures are provisional: the Panel will review them within 12 months, and in light of experience and comments received, will revise them if necessary; and will recommend to the Executive Directors ("Executive Directors") amendments to the Resolution that would allow a more effective role for the Panel.

Composition

The Panel consists of three Inspectors. At the outset, one Inspector, the Chairperson, will work on a full-time basis: the other two will work part-time. This arrangement is provisional. The Panel's workload will be dictated by the number and nature of requests received. If necessary, the Panel will recommend alternative arrangements to the Executive Directors.

Purpose

The Panel has been established for the purpose of providing people directly and adversely affected by a Bank-financed project with an independent forum through which they can request the Bank to act in accordance with its own policies and procedures. It follows that this forum is available when adversely affected people believe the Bank itself has failed, or has failed to require others, to comply with its policies and procedures, and only after efforts have been made to ask the Bank Management ("Management") itself to deal with the problem.

Functions

The role of the Panel is to carry out independent investigations. Its function, which will be triggered when it receives a request for inspection, is to inquire and recommend: it will make a preliminary review of a request for inspection and the response of Management, independently assess the information and then recommend to the Board of Executive Directors whether or not the matters complained of should be investigated. If the Board decides that a request shall be investigated, the Panel will collect information and provide its findings, independent assessment and conclusions to the Board. On the basis of the Panel's findings and Management's recommendations, the Executive Directors will consider the actions, if any, to be taken by the Bank.

Participants

During the preliminary review period--up to the time the Panel makes a recommendation to the Board on whether or not the matter should be investigated--the Panel will accept statements or evidence from (a) the Requester, i.e. either the affected people and/or their duly appointed representative, or an Executive Director; (b) Management; and, (c) any other individual or entity invited by the Panel to present information or comments.

During an investigation, any person who is either a party to the investigation or who provides the designated Inspector(s) with satisfactory evidence that he/she has an interest, apart from any interest in common with the public, will be entitled to submit information or evidence relevant to the investigation.

Administration

The Panel has approved separate Administrative Procedures which are available from the Office of The Inspection Panel.

(Please note that all headings are for ease of reference only. They do not form part of these procedures and do not constitute an interpretation thereof.)

SUBJECT MATTER OF REQUESTS

Scope

1. The Panel is authorized to accept requests for inspection ("Request(s)") which claim that an actual or threatened material adverse effect on the affected party's rights or interests arises directly out of an action or omission of the Bank as a result of a failure by the Bank to follow its own operational policies and procedures during the design, appraisal and/or implementation of a Bank financed project. Before submitting a Request steps must have already been taken (or efforts made) to bring the matter to the attention of Management with a result unsatisfactory to the Requester.

Limitations

2. The Panel is not authorized to deal with the following:

> (a) complaints with respect to actions which are the responsibility of other parties, such as the borrower, or potential borrower, and which do not involve any action or omission on the part of the Bank;
> (b) complaints against procurement decisions by Bank borrowers from suppliers of goods and services financed or expected to be financed by the Bank under a loan/credit agreement, or from losing tenderers for the supply of any such goods and services, which will continue to be addressed by Bank staff under existing procedures;
> (c) Requests filed after the Closing Date of the loan/credit financing the project with respect to which the Request is filed or when 95% or more of the loan/credit proceeds have been disbursed; or
> (d) Requests related to a particular matter or matters over which the Panel has already made its recommendation after having received a prior Request, unless justified by new evidence or circumstances not known at the time of the prior Request.

PREPARATION OF A REQUEST

3. The Panel's operational proceedings begin when a Request is received. This section of the procedures is primarily designed to give further guidance to potential Requesters on what facts and explanations they should provide.

A. Who Can File a Request

4. The Panel has authority to receive Requests which complain of a violation of the Bank's policies and procedures from the following people or entities:

> (a) any group of two or more people in the country where the Bank financed project is located who believe that as a result of the Bank's violation their rights or interests have been, or are likely to be adversely affected in a direct and material way. They may be an organization, association, society or other grouping of individuals; or
> (b) a duly appointed local representative acting on explicit instructions as the agent of adversely affected people; or
> (c) in exceptional cases, referred to in paragraph 11 below, a foreign representative acting as agent of adversely affected people; or
> (d) an Executive Director of the Bank in special cases of serious alleged violations of the Bank's policies and procedures.

B. Contents of a Request

5. In accordance with the Resolution, Requests should contain the following information:

> (a) a description of the project, stating all the relevant facts including the harm suffered by or threatened to the affected party;
> (b) an explanation of how Bank policies, procedures or contractual documents were seriously violated;
> (c) a description of how the act or omission on the part of the Bank has led or may lead to a violation of the specific provision;
> (d) a description of how the party was, or is likely to be, materially and adversely affected by the Bank's act or omission and what rights or interests of the claimant were directly affected;
> (e) a description of the steps taken by the affected party to resolve the violations with Bank staff, and explanation of why the Bank's response was inadequate;
> (f) in Requests relating to matters previously submitted to the Panel, a statement specifying what new evidence or changed circumstances justify the Panel revisiting the issue; and
> (g) if some of the information cannot be provided, an explanation should be included.

C. Form of Request

Written

6. All Requests must be submitted in writing, dated and signed by the Requester and contain his/her name and contact address.

Format

7. No specific form is necessary: a letter will suffice. A Requester may wish to refer to the guidance and use the model form specifying required information. [Attached]

Language

8. The working language of the Panel is English. Requests submitted directly by affected people themselves may be in their local language if they are unable to obtain a translation. If requests are not in English, the time needed to translate and ensure an accurate and agreed translation may delay acceptance and consideration by the Panel.

Representatives

9. If the Requester is a directly affected person or entity representing affected people, written signed proof that the representative has authority to act on their behalf must be attached.

10. If the Request is submitted by a non-affected representative, he/she must provide evidence of representational authority and the names and contact address of the party must be provided. Proof of representational authority, which shall consist of the original signed copy of the affected party's explicit instructions and authorization, must be attached.

11. In addition, in the cases of non-local representation, the Panel will require clear evidence that there is no adequate or appropriate representation in the country where the project is located.

Documents

12. The following documents should be attached:

    (a)   all correspondence with Bank staff;
    (b)   notes of meetings with Bank staff;
    (c)   a map or diagram, if relevant, showing the location of the affected party or area affected by the project; and
    (d)   any other evidence supporting the complaint.

13. If all the information listed cannot be provided an explanation should be included.

D. Delivery of Request

14. Requests must be sent by registered or certified mail or delivered by hand in a sealed envelope against receipt to the Office of The Inspection Panel at 1818 H Street, N.W., Washington, D.C. 20433, U.S.A. or to the Bank's resident representative in the country where the project is located. In the latter case, the resident representative shall, after issuing a receipt to the Requester, forward the Request to the Panel through the next pouch.

E. Advice on Preparation

15. People or entities seeking advice on how to prepare and submit a Request may contact the Office of The Inspection Panel, which will provide information or may meet and discuss the requirements with potential requesters.

PROCEDURES ON RECEIPT OF A REQUEST

16. When the Panel receives a Request the Chairperson, on the basis of the information contained in the Request, shall either promptly register the Request, or ask for additional information, or find the Request outside the Panel's mandate.

A. Register

17. If the request appears to contain sufficient required information the chairperson shall register the Request in the Panel Register; promptly notify the Requester, the Executive Directors and the Bank President ("President") of the registration; and transmit to the President a copy of the Request with the accompanying documentation, if any.

Contents of Notice

18. The notice of registration shall:

    (a) record that the Request is registered and indicate the date of the registration and dispatch of that notice;
    (b) the notice will include the name of the project, the country where the project is located, the name of the Requester unless anonymity is requested, and a brief description of the Request;
    (c) notify the Requester that all communications in connection with the Request will be sent to the address stated in the Request, unless another address is indicated to the Panel Secretariat; and
    (d) request Management to provide the Panel, within 21 days after receipt of the notice and Request, with written evidence that it has complied, or intends to comply with the Bank's relevant policies and procedures. The notice shall specify the due date of the response.

B. Request Additional Information

19. If the chairperson finds the contents of the Request or documentation on representation insufficient, he/she may ask the Requester to supply further information.

20. Upon receipt of a Request, the chairperson shall send a written acknowledgment to the Requester, and will specify what additional information is required.

21. The Chairperson may refuse to register a Request until all necessary information and documentation is filed.

C. Outside Scope

22. If the chairperson finds, that the matter is without doubt manifestly outside the Panel's mandate, he/she will notify the Requesters, of his/her refusal to register the Request and of the reasons therefor; this will include but not be

limited to the following types of communications:

(a) Requests which are clearly outside the Panel's mandate including those listed above at paragraph 2;

(b) Requests which do not show the steps taken or effort made to resolve the matter with Management;

(c) Requests from an individual or from a non-authorized representative of an affected party;

(d) any correspondence, including but not limited to letters, memoranda, opinions, submissions or requests on any matter within the Panel's mandate which are not requests for an inspection; and

(e) Requests that are manifestly frivolous, absurd or anonymous.

Records

23. The number of such Requests and communications received shall be noted in the Register on a quarterly basis and the yearly total included in the Annual Report.

D. Need for Review

24. In cases where additional information is required, or where it is not clear whether a Request is manifestly outside the Panel's mandate, the Chairperson shall designate a Panel member to review the Request.

E. Revised Request

25. If the Requester receives significant new evidence or information at any time after the initial Request was submitted, he/she may consider whether or not it is serious enough to justify the submission of a revised Request.

26. If a revised Request is submitted, the time periods for Management's response and the Panel recommendation will begin again from the time such Request is registered.

MANAGEMENT'S RESPONSE

27. Within 21 days after being notified of a Request, Management shall provide the Panel with evidence that it has complied, or intends to comply with the Bank's relevant policies and procedures. After the Panel receives Management's response, it shall promptly enter the date of receipt in the Panel Register.

28. If there is no response from Management within 21 days, the Panel shall notify the President and the Executive Directors and send a copy to the Requester.

Clarification

29. In order to make an informed recommendation, the Panel may request clarification from Management; in the light of Management's response, request more information from the Requester; and provide relevant portions of Management's response for comment. A time limit for receipt of the information requested shall be specified; and

(a) whether or not such clarification or information is received within the time limit, make its recommendation to the Executive Directors within 21 days after receipt of Management's response; or

(b) in the event it is not possible for the Requester to provide the information quickly, the Panel may advise the Requester to submit an amended Request; the Executive Directors and Bank management will be notified that the process will begin again when the amended Request is received.

PANEL RECOMMENDATION

30. Within 21 days after receiving Management's response, the Panel shall make a recommendation to the Executive Directors as to whether the matter should be investigated.

A. Basis

31. The Panel shall prepare its recommendation to the Board on the basis of the information contained in:

   (a) the Request;
   (b) Management's response;
   (c) any further information the Panel may have requested and received from the Requester and/or Management and/or third parties; and
   (d) any findings of the Panel during this stage.

B. Required Criteria

32. If, on the basis of the information contained in the Request, it has not already been established that the Request meets the following three conditions required by the Resolution, the Chairperson, in consultation with the other Panel members may, if necessary, designate a Panel member to conduct a preliminary review to determine whether the Request:

   (a) was filed by an eligible party;
   (b) is not time-barred; and
   (c) relates to a matter falling within the Panel's mandate.

Criteria for Satisfactory Response

33. The Panel may proceed to recommend that there should not be an investigation, if, on the basis of the information contained in the Request and Management's response, the Panel is satisfied that Management has done the following:

   (a) dealt appropriately with the subject matter of the Request; and
   (b) demonstrated clearly that it has followed the required policies and procedures; or
   (c) admitted that it has failed to follow the required policies and procedures but has provided a statement of specific remedial actions and a time-table for implementing them, which will, in the judgment of the Panel, adequately correct the failure and any adverse effects such failure has already caused.

ANNEX 4

Preliminary Review

34. If, on the basis of the information contained in Management's response and any clarifications provided, the Panel is satisfied that Management has failed to demonstrate that it has followed, or is taking adequate steps to follow the Bank's policies and procedures, the Panel will conduct a preliminary review in order to determine whether conditions required by provisions of the Resolution exist.

35. Although it may not investigate Management's actions in depth at this stage, it will determine whether Management's failure to comply with the Bank's policies and procedures meets the following three conditions:

    (a)   whether such failure has had, or threatens to have, a material adverse effect;
    (b)   whether, the alleged violation of the Bank's policies and procedures are, in the judgment of the Panel, of a serious character; and
    (c)   whether remedial actions proposed by Management do not appear adequate to meet the concerns of the Requester as to the application of the Bank's policies and procedures.

Initial Study

36. If the Chairperson considers, after the preliminary review and consultation with the other Panel members, that more factual data not already provided by the Requester, Management or any other source is required to make an informed recommendation to the Executive Directors, he/she may designate a Panel member to undertake a preliminary study. The study may include, but need not be limited to, a desk study and/or a visit to the project site.

C. Contents

37. On the basis of the review, the Panel shall make its recommendation to the Board as to whether the matter should be investigated. Every recommendation shall include a clear explanation setting forth reasons for the recommendation and be accompanied by:

    (a)   the text of the Request and, where applicable, any other relevant information provided by the Requester;
    (b)   the text of Management's response and, where applicable, any clarifications provided;
    (c)   the text of any advice received from the Bank's Legal Department;
    (d)   any other relevant documents or information received; and
    (e)   statements of the majority and minority views in the absence of a consensus by the Panel.

D. Submission

38. The recommendation shall be circulated by the Executive Secretary of the Panel to the Executive Directors for decision. The Panel will notify the Requester that a recommendation has been sent to the Executive Directors.

BOARD DECISION AND PUBLIC RELEASE

39. The Board decides whether or not to accept or reject the Panel's recommendation; and, if the Requester is a non-local representative, whether exceptional circumstances exist and suitable local representation is not available.

Notification

40. The Panel shall promptly inform the Requester of the Board's decision on whether or not to investigate the Request and, shall send the Requester a copy of the Panel's recommendation.

Public Information

41. After the Executive Directors have considered a Request the Bank shall make such Request publicly available together with the Panel's recommendation on whether to proceed with the inspection and the decision of the Executive Directors in this respect.

AN INVESTIGATION

A. Initial Procedures

42. When a decision to investigate a Request is made by the Board, or the Board itself requests an investigation, the Chairperson shall promptly:

> (a) designate one or more of the Panel's members (Inspector(s)) to take primary responsibility for the investigation;
> (b) arrange for the Panel members to consult, taking into account the nature of the particular Request, on:
>> (i) the methods of investigation that at the outset appear the most appropriate;
>> (ii) an initial schedule for the conduct of the investigation;
>> (iii) when the Inspector(s) shall report his/her (their) findings to the Panel, including any interim findings; and
>> (iv) any additional procedures for the conduct of the investigation.

43. The designated Inspector(s) shall, as needed, arrange for a meeting with the Requester and schedule discussions with directly affected people.

44. The name of the Inspector(s) and an initial work plan shall be made public as soon as possible.

B. Methods of Investigation

45. The Panel may, taking into account the nature of the particular Request, use a variety of investigatory methods, including but not limited to:

(a) meetings with the Requester, affected people, Bank staff, government officials and project authorities of the country where the project is located, representatives of local and international non-governmental organizations;

(b) holding public hearings in the project area;

(c) visiting project sites;

(d) requesting written or oral submissions on specific issues from the Requester, affected people, independent experts, government or project officials, Bank staff, or local or international non-governmental organizations;

(e) hiring independent consultants to research specific issues relating to a Request;

(f) researching Bank files; and

(g) any other reasonable methods the Inspector(s) consider appropriate to the specific investigation.

Consent Required

46. In accordance with the Resolution, physical inspection in the country where the project is located will be carried out with prior consent. The Chairperson shall request the Executive Director representing such country to provide written consent.

C. Participation of Requester

47. During the course of the investigation, in addition to any information requested by the Inspector(s), the Requester (and affected people if the Requester is a non-affected Representative or an Executive Director) or Bank staff may provide the Inspector(s) either directly or through the Executive Secretary with supplemental information that they believe is relevant to evaluating the Request.

48. The Inspector(s) may notify the Requester of any new material facts provided by Bank staff or by the Executive Director for, or authorities in the country where the project is located.

49. To facilitate understanding of specific points, the Panel may discuss its preliminary findings of fact with the Requester.

D. Participation of Third Parties

50. During the course of the investigation, in addition to any information requested by the Inspector(s), any member of the public may provide the Inspector(s), either directly or through the Executive Secretary, with supplemental information that they believe is relevant to evaluating the Request.

51. Information should not exceed ten pages and include a one-page summary. Supporting documentation may be listed and attached. The Inspector(s) may request more details if necessary.

PANEL REPORT

Contents

52. The report of the Panel (the "Report") shall include the following:

> (a) a summary discussion of the relevant facts and of the steps taken to conduct the investigation;
> (b) a conclusion showing the Panel's findings on whether the Bank has complied with relevant Bank policies and procedures;
> (c) a list of supporting documents which will be available on request from the Office of The Inspection Panel; and
> (d) statements of the majority and minority views in the absence of a consensus by the Panel.

Submission

53. Upon completion of the Report, the Panel shall submit it to:

> (a) the Executive Directors: accompanied by notification that the Report is being submitted to the President on the same date; and
> (b) the President: accompanied by a notice against receipt that within 6 weeks of receipt of the Report, Management must submit to the Executive Directors for their consideration a report indicating Management's recommendations in response to the Panel's findings.

MANAGEMENT'S RECOMMENDATIONS

54. Within 6 weeks after receiving the Panel's findings, Management will submit to the Executive Directors for their consideration a report indicating its recommendations in response to the Panel's findings. Upon receipt of a copy of the report, the Panel will notify the Requester.

BOARD DECISION AND PUBLIC RELEASE

55. Within 2 weeks after the Executive Directors consider the Panel's Report and the Management's response, the Bank shall inform the Requester of the results of the investigation and the action decided by the Board, if any.

56. After the Bank has informed the Requester, the Bank shall make publicly available:

> (a) the Panel's Report;
> (b) Management's recommendations; and
> (c) the Board's decision.

These documents will also be available at the Office of The Inspection Panel.

57. The Panel will seek to enhance public awareness of the results of investigations through all available information sources.

GENERAL

Business Days

58. "Days" under these procedures means days on which the Bank is open for business in Washington, D.C.

Copies

59. Consideration of Requests and other documents submitted throughout the process will be expedited if an original and two copies are filed. When any document contains extensive supporting documentation the Panel may ask for additional copies.

Consultations

60. The borrower and the Executive Director representing the borrowing (or guaranteeing) country shall be consulted on the subject matter before the Panel's recommendation and during an investigation.

Access to Bank Staff and Information

61. Pursuant to the Resolution and in discharge of their functions, the members of the Panel shall have access to all Bank staff who may contribute information and to all pertinent Bank records and shall consult as needed with the Director General, Operations Evaluation Department, and the Internal Auditor.

Legal Advice

62. The Panel shall seek, through the Vice President and General Counsel of the Bank, the written advice of the Bank's Legal Department on matters related to the Bank's rights and obligations with respect to the Request under consideration. Any such advice will be included as an attachment to the Panel's recommendation and/or Report to the Executive Directors.

Confidentiality

63. Documents, or portions of documents of a confidential nature will not be released by the Panel without the express written consent of the party concerned.

Information to Requester and Public

64. The Executive Secretary shall record in the Register all actions taken in connection with the processing of the Request, the dates thereof, and the dates on which any document or notification under these procedures is received in or sent from the Office of The Inspection Panel. The Requester shall be informed promptly. The Register will be publicly available.

65. A notice that a Request has been registered and all other notices or documents issued by the Panel will be available to the public through the Bank's PIC in Washington, D.C.; at the Bank's Resident Mission in the country where

the project is located or at the relevant regional office; at the Bank's Paris, London and Tokyo offices; or on request from the Executive Secretary of the Panel.

GUIDANCE ON HOW TO PREPARE A REQUEST FOR INSPECTION

The Inspection Panel needs some basic information in order to process a Request for Inspection:

1. Name, contact address and telephone number of the group or people making the request.

2. Name and description of the Bank project.

3. Adverse effects of the Bank project.

4. If you are a representative of affected people attach explicit written instructions from them authorizing you to act on their behalf.

These key questions must be answered:

1. Can you elaborate on the nature and importance of the damage caused by the project to you or those you represent?

2. Do you know that the Bank is responsible for the aspects of the project that has or may affect you adversely? How did you determine this?

3. Are you familiar with Bank policies and procedures that apply to this type of project? How do you believe the Bank may have violated them?

4. Have you contacted or attempted to contact Bank staff about the project? Please provide information about all contacts, and the responses, if any, you received from the Bank. You must have done this *before* you can file a request.

5. Have you tried to resolve your problem through any other means?

6. If you know that the Panel has dealt with this matter before, do you have new facts or evidence to submit?

Please provide a summary of the information in no more than a few pages. Attach as much other information as you think necessary as separate documents. Please note and identify attachments in your summary.

You may wish to use the attached model form.

ANNEX 4

MODEL FORM:
REQUEST FOR INSPECTION

To: The Executive Secretary
The Inspection Panel
1818 H St., NW, Washington, D.C. 20433, U.S.A.
(or to a World Bank Country/Regional Office

We,_____, and , and other persons whose names and addresses are attached live/represent others, living in the area known as: [and shown in the attached map or diagram] claim the following:

1. The Bank is financing the design/appraisal and/or implementation of a project [name and brief description]

2. We understand that the Bank has the following policy(ies) and/or procedures [list or describe]:

3. Our rights/interests are [describe]:

4. The Bank has violated its own policies/procedures in this way:

5. We believe our rights/interests have been, are likely to be adversely affected as a direct result of the Bank's violation. This is, or is likely to cause us to suffer [describe harm]:

6. We believe the action/omission is the responsibility of the Bank.

7. We have complained/made an effort to complain to Bank staff by [describe]:

Please attach evidence or explanation.

8. We received no response; or
We believe that the response(s) (attached/not attached) is unsatisfactory because:[describe why]:

9. In addition we have taken the following steps to resolve our problem:

We therefore believe that the above actions/omissions which are contrary to the above policies or procedures have materially and adversely affected our rights/interests and request the Panel to recommend to the Bank's Executive Directors that an investigation of these matters be carried out in order to resolve the problem.

As advised in your Operating Procedures, this Request for Inspection is brief. We can provide you with more particulars.

DATE: _____
SIGNATURES:_____
CONTACT ADDRESS: _____
_____
_____

Attachments: [Yes][No]
We authorize you to make this
Request public [Yes][No]

Annex 5

Panel Budget

The Inspection Panel Budget
Fiscal 2001
(thousands of U.S. dollars)

Fees - Panel Members	292.0
Salaries*	598.8
Temporaries	17.3
Consultants Short-term	97.9
Overtime	.3
Travel - Members/Staff	205.4
Benefits*	299.4
Communications and IT	49.4
Equipment & Building Services	6.1
Representation and Hospitality	4.9
Contractual Services	21.1
Other Expenses	73.3
Office Occupancy	142.8
Total Expenses	**1,809.0**
Current Budget	**2,099.8**

Note: Numbers may not add to totals because of rounding.
* Includes Chairman's salary.